D0833969

BER

Please renew or return items by the date
shown on your receipt

www.hertsdirect.org/libraries

Renewals and
enquiries: 0300 123 4049

Textphone for hearing   0300 123 4041
or speech impaired

H46 376 427 4

AMAZING & EXTRAORDINARY FACTS

JAMES BOND

AMAZING & EXTRAORDINARY FACTS

JAMES BOND

MICHAEL PATERSON

David and Charles

CONTENTS

INTRODUCTION

There are two 'James Bonds'. One is the hero of Ian Fleming's
novels; the other is the 007 of the cinema screen. The first
is fixed in time, a product of World War II, who lived in the
1950s and early 60s. He shared the class background, the war
experiences, the tastes and the general outlook of his creator.
He lived in a country still subject (in 1953) to rationing and
shortages – of money, housing, luxuries, good meals and elegant
clothes. Although he could enjoy these things, he paid for them
through the stress of his work, which was dirty and dangerous.
He was often exhausted, wounded or traumatised; he lacked
humour, and occasionally even confidence. He felt periodic
melancholy with his role and sometimes doubted whether the
West had any right to feel morally superior to its communist
enemy. He even, in one novel, 'shredded his nerves' with worry.

The Bond of the movies, who grew from this character, is not
stuck in a particular time. He belongs to the 1960s and to every
decade since, for he is continually reborn, recreated, replaced and
updated. He is never fazed by the unfamiliar or the threatening,
and never hesitates or wonders what to do. He is an expert on any

required subject and he has so much humour that his conversation sometimes consists of little else. He is a more reckless driver than his counterpart, he travels more widely, he seduces more women and he kills more men. His gadgetry is more extensive and more elaborate. He is an entirely different person, and he is far better known. More of us have seen him on screen, in one or other of his six personifications, than will ever read books about him – indeed it is estimated that over half the world's population have watched at least one of his movies. It is of the cinema Bond that we automatically think when we conjure up an image of 007.

From time to time there are attempts to make the movie Bond more ordinary, more like the Bond of the novels, or more in keeping with contemporary attitudes and expectations. Perhaps he drinks and smokes less, or not at all. He is less fastidious, more casual in dress, he is less 'posh' – although care is taken that his attitude to women remains cheerfully behind the times. Such a makeover has happened most recently when Daniel Craig took over the role. Although he is far less polished than Fleming would probably have wished, he has won praise from serious fans for portraying 007 in a manner more faithful to the original.

The women too have changed. To begin with they were more helpless, more in need of protection, more adoring. Not all, admittedly, were this type – one thinks of Tracy di Vincenzo in *On Her Majesty's Secret Service*, or the Havelock daughter in *For Your Eyes Only*. These days, however, the women are independent, invulnerable, more skilled, less willing to be rescued, more likely to help defeat the enemy, and more resentful of Bond's attitude toward them. Although Bond and the Bond women have changed, the villains have remained much the same. They are uniformly wealthy, deranged, physically abnormal, charming and surprisingly patient, considering the frequency with which 007 irritates and frustrates them.

Modernised and reinterpreted for each new generation, Bond has outlasted his original context – a grim and austere post-war world in the grip of East-West confrontation – and is even more popular in the new era of affluence and global terrorism. Why has he proved so durable? And why do people all over the world enjoy the adventures of what one American called a 'Limey cop'?

The reasons are four-fold. Firstly, because the themes are universal, an audience in any country can enjoy the agent's hair's-breadth escapes and feel relief when he outwits an assassin or dispatches an undesirable. If Bond is the projection of a typical middle-aged man's fantasies, such men are to be found all over the globe. Secondly, the movies are completely international in their settings, casting and situations, and only some of the characters are British – the villains, of course, virtually never are. Thirdly, Britain has a small but highly professional movie industry. The facilities and crews are excellent, and now have decades of experience in making Bond movies. This technical expertise means that the movies are visually spectacular. And fourthly, many worldwide viewers have stereotyped notions of the English, and enjoy seeing these brought to the screen in the shape of M, Q, and Bond himself.

Any audience can enjoy the escapism offered by the world of Bond. He is what so many of us would want to be: invincible, bereft of doubts or hang-ups, and with the lifestyle of the international rich. At first, in his early years, he was envied because he could travel without restriction to places that were beyond the reach of most. He could dine on food that was unfamiliar, expensive and un-rationed. He could spend other people's money (the government's) and, most importantly perhaps, he could have sex with virtually any woman he met.

Now millions can live something of the James Bond lifestyle. Pleasures that once seemed unattainable have been brought within our reach by a rising standard of living, more and better restaurants, budget airlines, and the contraceptive pill. Yet Bond still remains above and beyond the broad mass of humanity because he is untroubled by everyday concerns, and he remains refreshingly aloof from the cares that preoccupy others. We never see him queuing in shops, paying a fine because his car has been clamped, or having his clothes ruined in the wash. He has no wife to nag him, no children to go off the rails because he was not there during the crucial years of their adolescence. He does not have to pay alimony, or struggle to afford school fees. He is never, in fact, short of money or financially embarrassed. His problems – and they are serious enough, goodness knows – involve saving his life, saving the heroine, saving the country or indeed the world, but otherwise he never experiences even the difficulty of having to look for a parking space. And every time he starts to get too old to chase villains or seduce women he is replaced by a younger, fitter version of himself and carries on. Who would not dream of being this man?

This is a book for all those who enjoy – without taking too seriously – the novels of Ian Fleming and his numerous successors, as well as the movies they have inspired. While I was typing this text, my mind filled with phrases like 'Licence to Kill' and 'Licence Regained'. The anti-virus protection on my computer apparently ran out for, up on the screen, flashed the words YOUR LICENCE HAS EXPIRED. Can I suggest this as a title for the last-ever Bond movie, with the hope that it will not be made for a very long time to come?

'The name's Bond, James Bond …'
A name 'as ordinary as possible'

Physically, James Bond is effectively his creator, Ian Fleming (1908–1964), projected onto a larger screen. The description of 007 is broadly similar to that of the author, with the addition of a scar to suggest Bond's adventurous past. Fleming was, admittedly, slightly older than his character – 007 is in his mid-30s, while his creator was 43 at the outset, but this is a minor point. Fleming did not specify that he himself was the model for 007, but the similarities were obvious to those around him, and did no harm to the author's image or his sales. In terms of character, Fleming had had no difficulty crafting the personality of Bond from a number of men he had known during the war – commandos, naval officers and agents.

Finding the right name was somewhat trickier. Fleming's first choice had been frankly ludicrous; Peregrine Maltravers. This was far too cumbersome, and sounded hopelessly old-fashioned – a reflection of the Bulldog Drummond era of the 1920s in which lay the roots of Fleming's inspiration. He needed something that would fit into the contemporary world more easily, and that was both slick and bland. When in 1953 he was writing the first of the novels, *Casino Royale*, at his desk in Jamaica, his glance fell on a nearby book. It happened to be the *Field Guide to Birds of the West Indies,* by James Bond. According to Fleming legend, the author immediately borrowed the name and found that it perfectly suited his purpose.

There are other explanations for this name. In 1945 Fleming, still working in London for naval intelligence, was already thinking of writing a book. In conversation about this with his friend C.H. Forster, Forster asked how Fleming thought of names for his characters. Fleming explained that it was relatively easy; he would think of the first couple of names of the boys in his house at school and swap their Christian names. In his case, Forster said, the first names were James Aitken and Harry Bond; this meant that the result would be Harry

Aitken and James Bond. Apparently Fleming had felt that James Bond sounded the better of the two.

In addition, one of the rugged wartime acquaintances on whom his hero was to be modelled had been a friend of Fleming's brother Peter, a commando named Rodney Bond. 'James Bond' might in any case have seemed familiar – the sort of name one would feel one had heard before. In fact it had already been used for a character in a short story by Agatha Christie called *The Rajah's Emerald* published in 1934, and St James Bond is even the name of a church in Toronto, Canada.

The name quickly came to seem the only suitable one for Fleming's suave and ruthless creation. The author wanted a name that was 'as ordinary as possible', and later explained that it seemed to him this choice was brief and unromantic, Anglo Saxon and yet very masculine – exactly what the character needed. Neither Fleming nor his early readers could have had any notion of just how romantic it would eventually become in the minds of the public.

As a courtesy, Fleming contacted the name's real owner to see if he had any objection to its use, although only after he had begun using it. The true James Bond, an American from Philadelphia, though educated at Harrow and Cambridge in England, was a highly respected museum ornithologist. He replied that he was 'fine with it', and that was that. The two men met for lunch during the last months of Fleming's life at Goldeneye, and Fleming sent Bond a first edition of his novel *You Only Live Twice*. The inscription, to the 'real James Bond', was from 'the thief of his identity'.

The 'real' James Bond died, aged 89, in 1989. Despite his generosity in lending his name, one wonders if he ever got used to the hilarity that must have greeted him every time he tried to book a restaurant table!

The man with the golden typewriter
The life and inspirations of Ian Fleming

Ian Lancaster Fleming was born in 1908, the second of four sons. His family, astute and thrifty Scottish merchants, had made enough money in the nineteenth century to be able to afford the trappings of gentility and to move in London society. This branch of the Flemings was well-off but not conspicuously wealthy. His father, apart from serving in the family firm, was the Tory MP for Henley and a friend of Winston Churchill. His mother was a formidable woman who, like Churchill's own mother, would use her considerable social influence to advance her son's progress.

Ian was educated at Eton, where he

was overshadowed by his brilliant elder brother, Peter. Ian's only achievement – and it was not inconsiderable – was to be the school's *Victor Ludorum*, or overall sports champion, two years in a row; he remained proud of this all his life. He then attended the Royal Military Academy Sandhurst, although he did not complete the course or receive a commission. He also failed the entrance exams for the Foreign Office. At a loose end, he was sent to a finishing school of sorts in the Austrian Alps, and he also lived briefly in Geneva. From this phase of his life he gained experiences – of skiing and mountaineering, and of driving fast cars across Europe – that would influence the character of Bond.

Back in London Fleming was able, through his mother's connections, to join Reuters Agency. Languid by nature and not keen on hard work, he nevertheless became an extremely competent journalist. His brief career with the agency taught him to write quickly and to the point. When he began the Bond books he was to compose directly onto the typewriter without making notes in longhand. He was also to create – and maintain – a strict daily regimen of work, producing a set number of words each day. Reuters gave him the sense of professional discipline that enabled him to produce a novel a year for over a decade. The agency also sent him abroad to cover particular events and he visited Russia on two occasions during the 1930s – trips that would later enhance his descriptions of the country and its people in his novels.

Needing a larger income to finance the life he was leading, Fleming changed career and became a stockbroker. He was not a very good one, although the remuneration enabled him to live in some style in central London, to collect rare books (as well as pornography) and to play innumerable golf matches. Charming, and well aware of being handsome, he

also devoted a great deal of time and energy to seduction. Understandably there are distinct similarities between Fleming's attitude to sex and that of his fictional counterpart.

With the outbreak of World War II Fleming was taken on, by personal recommendation, as Assistant to Rear Admiral Sir John Godfrey, the Director of Naval Intelligence. Based at the Admiralty in London, the two worked well together until Godfrey left the post. Gruff, demanding, bad-tempered but avuncular, character traits of Fleming's former boss would emerge largely unaltered in the character of M in the Bond stories.

Fleming loved his work at the Admiralty, which included devising schemes to put agents into occupied Europe, or to deceive the enemy. Fleming himself was keen to take part in some of the expeditions he planned, but because of his access to sensitive information he could not be put at risk of capture. He spent the war largely in Whitehall, although he accompanied the Dieppe Raid and undertook dangerous travel abroad. Setting up an intelligence-gathering commando unit, he came to know the world of espionage and the men – tough, individualistic and often eccentric – that peopled it.

WARTIME GADGETRY

Some of the gadgetry developed for Bond is criticised for implausibility, but it is worth recalling that in the shadowy world of wartime espionage, gadgets were frequently used for deception and sabotage, and were often thoroughly bizarre. One proposed example – never used, as far as is known – was an explosive booby-trap disguised as a dead rat for use by the French Resistance.

World War II gave Fleming two other experiences that proved valuable. Travelling in neutral Portugal, he spent an evening gambling for high stakes at a casino in Estoril. This scene – of apparent gaiety in the midst of war – provided the background idea for *Casino Royale*, and while attending an international conference in Jamaica in 1942, he discovered a love of the island that would last the rest of his life. He conceived at once an ambition to live there when the war was over, and

he was to do so – buying a parcel of land in 1946 and building a house upon it. Jamaica would provide not only the setting for his writing career but for novels and movies.

Fleming's post-war job was a dream. He was offered a position as Foreign Manager for the Kemsley group of newspapers. Based in the environs of Fleet Street, he was not only well paid for largely undemanding work but was allowed a staggering two months of holiday each year. This he took in the early months of the year, and it was in this annual gap period that he would write his novels.

Ian Fleming painted by Constance Vlahoulis

He conducted an affair with Ann Rothermere, the wife of a press baron, and following her divorce he married her. He was 43 years old and, as a lifelong bachelor, was somewhat panic-stricken at the thought of matrimony. He arrived in Jamaica, in February 1952, not only with an idea for a book but with something of a mid-life crisis. He felt he had achieved nothing, and he was still as overshadowed by his elder brother as he had been at school. This was his state of mind when he began to type the manuscript that was to become *Casino Royale*.

After a slow start the book began to sell well, and the following year he wrote another, *Live and Let Die*, this time with a Caribbean rather than a European setting. The novels picked up momentum and editions began to sell out within months of publication. Fleming was becoming a power in the literary world, although his wife and her intellectual friends despised his work. An endorsement from President Kennedy, who enjoyed the novels as well as the release in 1962 of the first Bond movie, *Dr No*, catapulted Fleming's sales into the stratosphere. For 12 years he would produce a novel annually, although his health, and his imagination, would gradually decline.

Fleming was a habitual smoker and drinker, and refused to moderate his habits. They were intrinsic to his lifestyle, and he would continue to enjoy his vices and make no attempt to lengthen his life by curbing them. In keeping with this attitude, he shrugged off medical advice and his physical decline gathered pace. At the age of 38 doctors had warned that he was putting too much strain on his heart and body. By the time he was in his mid-50s, with a heart attack already behind him, he was visibly ailing. In 1964, he typed – slowly – his last novel, *The Man With the Golden Gun*. Soon afterward he had to be hospitalised after catching a cold. He developed pleurisy, was found to have a blockage of the pulmonary artery and, some months later, died of a second and bigger heart attack. He was 56 years old.

WHO INSPIRED BOND?

A largely forgotten English novelist, Phyllis Bottome (1884–1963), met Ian Fleming when he was 19 years old and encouraged him to write. A well-known personality in her day, Bottome was a writer and hostess with a large international circle of friends. Her first novel was titled **Life the Interpreter** *(1902), and her best-known work was* **Old Wine** *(1926). Fleming never forgot that it was Bottome who had lit the spark of literary aspiration by praising a rather mediocre piece of work he had produced. This was a short story about a sadistic and womanising aristocrat called Graf Schlik, who in some ways was an embryonic Bond villain.*

In his elder brother's shadow
The distinguished career of Peter Fleming

Although the Bond novels have far outsold them, the books written by Ian Fleming's older brother Peter (1907–1971) were also bestsellers. An accomplished journalist, Peter wrote travel narratives that are still in print today, and until the mid-1950s he was far better known as a writer than Ian. He also had a more adventurous life than his sibling. His exploits and success spurred on his younger brother's efforts, and in some measure Peter was one of the inspirations for the Bond character.

Peter Fleming was born in 1907, almost exactly a year before Ian. While the younger boy made little academic impact, the elder had a distinguished career both in school and beyond. Handsome and charming, he went from Eton, where he was Editor of the school newspaper, to Christ Church, Oxford, where he took a First in English; during World War II he served in the Grenadier Guards. Peter married

Celia Johnson, the movie actress whose most memorable role was that of Laura Jesson in David Lean's movie *Brief Encounter* (1945).

In 1932 Peter Fleming embarked on an expedition up the Taprape River in Brazil after answering an advertisement in *The Times*. This gave him the material for a classic and exciting travel memoir, *Brazilian Adventure*, that was well received and can still be found in bookshops today. As a Special Correspondent for *The Times*, he subsequently travelled to Peking on the Orient Express. Two further works, *One's Company* and *News from Tartary*, written in 1936 and describing his wanderings in Central Asia, enhanced his reputation not only as a gifted writer but as a gentleman-adventurer.

With the coming of World War II, Peter found himself involved in organising the covert resistance groups that would carry out sabotage and guerrilla warfare following an anticipated German conquest of Britain. He also saw action in Norway, Greece and the Pacific, where he was in charge of a unit carrying out acts of military deception.

After the war, he retired to become a country gentleman in Oxfordshire. He wrote two accounts of the planned Nazi attack on Britain, *Operation Sea Lion* and *Invasion 1940*, titles that are now recognised as classics. Publishers had been reluctant to consider his brother's first novel, *Casino Royale*, and it was only through Peter's connection with London publishing house Jonathan Cape that the novel eventually came to print. Outliving his brother by several years, Peter sat on the board of Glidrose Productions Ltd, the company that controlled the rights to the Bond 'brand'.

Father figure
The heroic Valentine Fleming

I an Fleming's father died when the boy was nine years old, yet he was another family figure who greatly influenced the young author. As an officer in the Queen's Own Oxfordshire Hussars, Major Valentine Fleming became a heroic figure in World War I and was killed in action, near St Quentin on the Western Front, in May 1917.

Despite his family's Scottish origins, Valentine had been brought up as an archetypal English gentleman. His dynasty had established a merchant bank that still flourishes today, and this enabled his family to live in some style, with houses in Mayfair in London, and in the country. Although he was no intellectual, Valentine had the skill at games, the sense of basic decency, and the willingness to join public service that was to characterise the English upper class at the time.

Valentine attended Eton College, where he rowed for the school and belonged to 'Pop', the prestigious prefectorial society. He achieved a degree in History at Magdalen College, Oxford, and read Law, although he never actually practised it. Instead he worked for the family bank, and in 1910 he defeated the Liberal incumbent to become the Conservative MP for Henley, an Oxfordshire town near his family's estate.

Valentine spoke in the Commons in favour of National Service, and endorsed his convictions by serving in the Territorial Army. It is interesting to learn that his comrades in the Queen's Own Oxfordshire Hussars included Winston and Jack Churchill. Winston, at the time a Liberal MP and First Lord of the Admiralty, ensured that when war broke out in August 1914 the Regiment was among the first – and best-equipped – units to serve in France.

Away from home most of the time, Valentine was a remote presence to his four sons, although he wrote letters to them at their prep school describing his experiences in the trenches. He was to survive almost exactly three years on the Western Front, but one early summer's day, while crawling from one position to another opposite the Hindenburg Line, he was killed instantly by an exploding shell.

Churchill wrote the officer a fulsome obituary, which was published in *The Times*. Describing Valentine's personality as lovable and charming, Churchill – himself a man of strong passions – expressed admiration for his comrade's comparative moderation and for the thoughtfulness and tolerance of his opinions, which were strongly held although not loudly or forcibly expressed.

Valentine's sons were taught to revere his memory even to the extent of asking, in their regular family prayers, to grow up to be more like him. There can be no question that he was a strong influence on the life of Ian who, until his own death, kept a copy of Churchill's obituary for his father, framed and signed by Churchill himself, in his home.

Goldeneye
Fleming's dream house

Fleming first visited Jamaica during World War II in order to attend an Anglo-American naval conference in Kingston. Jamaica is not a difficult place to love at first sight, and Fleming was completely smitten. After years of wartime drabness, the colour and vitality of the island enchanted him. Jamaica was at that time a colonial backwater and completely undeveloped in terms of tourism. It was only during the 1950s when it was discovered by the international rich that its north shore would become fashionable – and prohibitively expensive. At the time this meant that, for a modest outlay,

Fleming was able to purchase a piece of land overlooking the sea and next to a former donkey-racing track.

On this spot he built a plain – indeed spartan – bungalow which he named 'Goldeneye'. Here he spent his two-month annual leave that he always took between January and March – perhaps the months that saw the worst British weather. Whatever sophistication he may have displayed at the gaming table, Fleming had little interest in cuisine. He did not cook more than basic dishes himself and the meals prepared by his Jamaican cook, Violet, were apparently so abominable that Noel Coward, a neighbour and frequent guest at Fleming's house, used to cross himself before eating.

Fleming had built the house in order to swim and write. It was

Jamaica

situated above a small and secluded beach that allowed him to bathe and snorkel whenever he wished. He also had a pool built beside the house, which originally comprised only three rooms. It was in one of these, his bedroom, that he sat down at a Royal portable typewriter one morning in February 1952 and began to work on the novel *Casino Royale*. He did not have extensive piles of notes, but he had been turning the plot over in his mind for so long that he had well-formed notions of what he wanted to write.

Thereafter, he stuck to a strict regime. Mornings were for work, afternoons for recreation. After breakfast, at about 9 o'clock each morning, he would close the wooden window shutters, blocking out the tropical sunlight, the sight of flowers and of birds, and immerse himself in his text. His target was 2,000 words a day, and he would work for three hours without stopping. At noon he would emerge, to lunch, sleep and swim. Returning at 5 o'clock in the evening, he would read through the morning's work, make whatever corrections occurred to him, and then put the manuscript in the left-hand bottom drawer of the roll-top desk at which he worked. And so it was that in the space of a month, every year for 12 years, he wrote a Bond novel.

ORIGINS OF THE NAME

The origins of the name for Fleming's residence have proved intriguing and there are three possibilities for the source: firstly the neighbouring headland, Orchabessa, translates as 'Golden Head'; secondly 'Operation Goldeneye' was the code name for a plan formulated by Fleming during the war; and thirdly, the name may have been a reference to a book Fleming enjoyed, **Reflections in a Golden Eye,** *by Carson McCullers.*

Goldeneye became legendary, as the place in which Bond was conceived, as the place in which a glamorous writer and his equally glamorous friends escaped the rigours of a northern winter while their compatriots shivered at home, and as the place to which the British Prime Minister, Anthony Eden, retreated in 1956 after his health broke down

Anthony Eden

following the Suez debacle. The British press in fact reported that the PM's three-week stay was disturbed by rodents and that Eden himself had joined in a rat hunt.

Ann Fleming was considerably less fond of Goldeneye than her husband. After his death in 1964 she had no wish to continue the routine of visits he had established. The house was left to Fleming's son, Caspar, but he died in 1975. The son of Fleming's friend Blanche, Chris Blackwell, record-label founder and owner of

resort hotels, now owns Goldeneye. Blackwell has made the house and its 52 acres of grounds into a discreet hotel and he has tried hard, and with success, to retain the atmosphere of the bungalow itself. Potential guests will be relieved to know that the food is much better than in the days of Violet. There are pleasant walks among the trees, in fact several of those same trees were planted by famous guests: the Clintons, Grace Jones, Piers Brosnan – and the Edens, who started the tradition. There are cabins in the grounds, and the rooms in these are named after the heroines of the stories – Honeychile, Vesper, Tiffany, Domino, Solitaire… In the main house, the three rooms are numbered instead – 007, 008 and 009. Room 007 is Fleming's old bedroom, and his famous roll-top desk is still to be found here.

Unlikely scenario
Fleming's 'steely patriotism'

Fleming was intensely proud of Britain. His 'steely patriotism', about which he had absolutely no sense of humour, was remarked upon by at least one American acquaintance. To someone of his class and background the sharp decline in Britain's status after 1945 was a matter of bewilderment and horror. Even before the end of World War II, the US and Russia were allowing Britain to join them in the Great Powers Club only as a courtesy. Humiliations followed one after another in the two decades after World War II as Britain withdrew from her Empire, bungled the Suez operation and faced a series of public scandals that completely undermined confidence in the establishment. The exposure of high-profile traitors – Burgess and McLean – made Britain's allies deeply suspicious and reluctant to share intelligence.

Fleming's personal antidote to this was pure wishful thinking. In 007 he created a parallel, fictional world in which Britain not only operated as an equal partner in the Cold War but actually dominated the US. Although Bond regards Felix Leiter, the US agent in the stories, as a great friend, this CIA officer never matches Bond's own wits or abilities. Leiter seems content to act as second fiddle to a British agent in the Caribbean (regarded by the US as its strategic backyard) and even on US soil.

In reality the US would not, by virtue of its power and resources, have been willing to take a secondary role in any situation, or to have a single and largely unarmed foreign operative take on numerous and well-organised enemies. The US FBI, and certainly not the British MI6, would have dealt

with the troublesome Spangled Mob or Goldfinger. Fleming, through his writings, was able to perpetuate the myth of British power and influence for years after these had waned.

BANG ON TIME

The success of the movies resulted not only from their combination of sex, violence and glamour but from the fact that the first releases fitted perfectly with the aspirations of the British public at that time. They loved the implication that their country could still take on, and defeat, more powerful enemies – making up in initiative, intelligence and courage what they lacked in resources. Terence Young, who directed the early movies, was to later say of them that he felt they had arrived not only in the right year, but also in the right week and the right month. The first of them, **Dr No,** *was released on 5 October 1962 and made £60 million at the box office.*

Amalgamation of daydreams
The similarities between Fleming and Bond

Fleming initially sought to make the character of James Bond an 'empty vessel', without tastes or opinions. He was to remark that his intention was to invent a hero with no characteristics, who simply operated as what he called a blunt instrument at the behest of the government. In writing about Bond, however, he began to endow him with his own interest in food, drink, clothes and women. As a result, his hero became synonymous with sophistication (not to mention a certain overt snobbishness) as well as adventure, and this greatly increased his popular appeal.

Fleming admitted that similarities were unavoidable as his agent began to eat and to dress in a certain way, gradually assuming a personality that the writer's friends recognised as the author's own. Fleming also revealed that his fictional hero was a means of living the life he himself would have wanted. He actually referred to one novel, on completing it, as the latest chapter of his autobiography.

These similarities between himself and his creation naturally made it easier to write the books, and lent them an unmistakable authenticity. Fleming, however, played down any physical or temperamental similarity between himself and Bond, saying that apart from the fact that they wore the same type of clothes they had little in common, and that although there were certainly things he envied in 007 – his efficiency and his blondes (his success with women was, after all, even more legendary than Fleming's own) – he did not much like him.

Nevertheless there can be little doubt that Fleming relished their common characteristics. He described his books as fairy tales for adults, and one critic less charitably wrote that they were the pillow fantasies of an adolescent mind. Perhaps so, but they were fantasies shared by a significant number of others. Another observer commented that Bond represented an amalgamation of all the daydreams of not only Fleming himself but also several million other men from all over the world.

A significant number
The origins of the highly-resonant 007

I an Fleming regularly spent his weekends in England golfing near the picturesque town of Sandwich on the Kent coast. Locals there believe that 007 – Bond's highly-resonant service number that signifies that he is 'licensed to kill' – was derived not from some inside knowledge of the workings of MI6 but was, in fact, inspired by a local bus as this is

the number of the National Express coach that runs between London and the east of Kent.

Leaving Victoria Coach Station – a stone's throw from Fleming's old London home in Victoria Square – the bus takes the same route that Fleming would have covered by car, and he must often have passed these vehicles on the road. Following the main road from London to Canterbury, the 007 bus then carries on to Dover and Folkestone, passing St Margaret's Bay, the setting for the novel *Moonraker* and a place where Fleming had often visited his friend Noel Coward. The number 007 can still be seen on the destination boards of coaches that make this journey.

Although this makes a good story, it is unlikely to be the complete picture. It has been suggested that two '0's – the symbol of a pair of eyes – were used as far back as Elizabethan times to signify that a document sent to the Queen was for her eyes only. The figures 00 were also employed by the German Diplomatic Service during World War I to indicate that a message was of the highest secrecy. This became an

important and well-known fact after German attempts to make an alliance with Mexico against the US – the so-called 'Zimmermann Telegram' affair – was revealed in 1917.

Zimmermann, the German Foreign Minister, sent a coded signal to his country's ambassador in Mexico, ordering him to approach the government there and propose the alliance. The ambassador was to offer as inducement the prospect that after a victorious war and a forced peace settlement, Mexico would be able to claim large tracts of territory from the South-Western US. When the message was decoded by British Intelligence and made public, American opinion turned overwhelmingly against Germany, and the US entered the war on the side of the Allies shortly afterwards. The telegram – one of the most infamous and best-known secret messages in history, and one that represented the greatest coup of the war for British decoders – had been prefixed 0075. Fleming was to disclose that the same prefix had been used for a time while he was working in naval intelligence during the war.

The probability therefore is that, like so much about the world of James Bond, there was no single inspiration or explanation for what the author conceived. One thing will have reminded Fleming of another – a newly-acquired fact or story waking echoes of other information half lost in memory. It is very likely that, seeing a London-bound bus with its distinctive number while driving to Kent one day, he would have been struck by its resemblance to a familiar secret code.

THE 00 SECTION

This small, fictional and presumably elite section of the British Secret Service varies in size according to circumstances or the whims of Bond novelists and scriptwriters, and in later novels it is threatened with disbandment as part of government cuts. Bond's 00 colleagues tend to be heard of only when they are in trouble, and they have little function other than to be killed off. The death of one, early in the plot, is a useful way of establishing the ruthlessness of a villain and of setting the scene for Bond to seek revenge.

Out of puff
Fleming runs short of inspiration

There came a point when Fleming confessed that he did not have enough ideas – or sufficient personal experiences to draw upon – to keep his series continuing indefinitely. After the seventh novel, *Thunderball*, he felt he had 'run out of puff' and had little more to offer. He subsequently went on to produce a further five novels – including one, *The Man With the Golden Gun*, that was published after his death, but fans consider these of lesser quality.

He had based his characters on a combination of people he knew or had heard about. Likewise his settings were the fruit of both personal travels, for business or pleasure, and specially undertaken research trips. He was, in other words, trying insofar as his health and other commitments allowed, to keep the flame of inspiration alight throughout his later years. He clearly did not lack the imagination necessary to think up plots, but perhaps felt that these were becoming weaker as his series progressed.

AN INTERNATIONAL POLICEMAN?

Fleming had decided by the turn of the 1960s that the East-West confrontation was less of a useful theme than international crime, a subject with which he confessed to being fascinated. In the stories – both as novels and movies – Bond becomes increasingly deployed as an international policeman and less as a secret agent against the Soviet Union. That is effectively what he has remained ever since.

The world is not enough
Who were James Bond's forebears?

Although considered an archetypal Englishman, Bond is in fact half Scottish and half Swiss. His father, an engineer, came from Glencoe in the Highlands – although the Bonds are not a Scottish clan and Bond is not a common Scots surname. On his mother's side his family were French-speaking Swiss, the Delacriox, from the Canton of Vaud. Both Scottish Highlanders and Swiss are regarded as dour, austere and simple-living peoples and it is difficult to imagine more inappropriate – or less believable – ancestors for the sybaritic secret agent. It is, incidentally, unlikely that Bond would hold dual citizenship. In the world of espionage this would pose a security risk, and he would therefore have had to renounce any claim to a Swiss passport.

Both Bond's parents perished in a climbing accident when he was 11 years old and in this Fleming's character follows a long tradition in adventure novels. For fictional heroes who require the image of a rugged loner, such circumstances are almost compulsory – there has

to be a clear-out of inconvenient relatives so that such men can have the necessary brooding, solitary and perhaps embittered nature (they usually learn not to become too attached to others as a result, which justifies their later cavalier treatment of women). Admittedly the notion of Bond having to visit his aged mother in a nursing home – or, worse, have her come to live with him – would detract from the machismo that his fans so much enjoy.

Bond himself has no interest in his ancestry. When paying a visit to the College of Arms in the novel *On Her Majesty's Secret Service* to investigate its dealings with Ernst Blofeld, he is lectured about his own family name. Griffin Or, one of the picturesquely-named officials on the staff, mistakenly assumes he is pursuing his own genealogical researches, and is surprised by his lack of enthusiasm, asking if he is not excited by the possibility that he might be descended from the man after whom one of the most famous streets in the world – London's Bond Street – is named. In Georgian times Bond Street was a fashionable promenade, and since the

eighteenth century it has been known for elegant shopping. Sotheby's and Bonham's, the auctioneers, as well as Asprey's, the jewellers, are situated there. As a name therefore, Bond Street is as synonymous with glamour as is 007 himself.

Although the thought of such a pedigree may have intrigued some readers none of this impresses 007, an unsentimental man who is, in any case, preoccupied with tracking his opponent. He shows interest only when told that the family crest includes three 'besants' or golden balls, and he comments drily that this is quite a bonus. During this conversation, the Bond family motto is revealed: 'The World is Not Enough'. This would come to provide the title for one of the later movies.

GENEALOGY AND BOND

The College of Arms, a very respected body that is the highest authority on matters of heraldry in Britain and elsewhere, has its headquarters on London's Queen Victoria Street, on a site it has occupied since 1555. Its elegant building, dating from the early eighteenth century, is briefly seen in the movie **On Her Majesty's Secret Service** *with Bond's car outside. However concerned it is with important matters of genealogy, the College has not forgotten its connection with the world's most famous secret agent; among the souvenirs that its visitors can buy are copies of the novel.*

School for spies
The Eton of the North

Like his creator Bond went to school at Eton although, according to the obituary of him that appears in the novel *You Only Live Twice*, he lasted only two terms there. He received the rest of his education at Fettes College in Edinburgh, Scotland, his father's old school. Sometimes known as 'the Eton of the North,' Fettes is arguably Scotland's best-known school. Founded in 1870 by a local merchant, its vast and distinctive main building is a familiar part of the Edinburgh skyline. In the 1930s it was famous for a cult of athletics (it still produces Scottish rugby internationals) and this suited Bond's temperament. He twice represented Fettes as a lightweight boxer, and founded 'the first serious judo class at a British public school'.

Fettes is aware – and probably rather proud – of its link with the fictional adventurer. It has, however, produced several real ones; it even had a pupil called James Bond who later served with the elite Special Boat Squadron. Other alumni include Nicholas Hammond (1907–2001), a brilliant classical scholar, who was parachuted into wartime Greece to train resistance fighters and became an expert in sabotage, winning the Distinguished Service Order. Also Robert Bruce Lockhart (1887–1987), who was to run Britain's propaganda effort in World War II, acted as a secret agent in Bolshevik Russia after the Revolution and was involved in a plot to rescue Tsar Nicholas II. Imprisoned in the Kremlin and condemned to death, he was exchanged for a Soviet spy. His book *Memoirs of a British Agent* became an international bestseller.

Fleming will have been aware of these men's background when drafting Bond's obituary, which he checked for plausibility with an Old Fettesian. However suitable Fettes may have been considered as a nursery for spies, it has plenty of other claims to fame. The school, now mixed, educated both the actress Tilda Swinton and the former British Prime Minister Tony Blair.

Precocious youth
Bond matures early

In order to have worked his way through all the past experiences attributed to him by his creator, James Bond would have had to start his life as a secret agent before World War II at about the age of 16. This was the scenario adopted by both Ian Fleming in his novels, and John Pearson in the latter's fictitious biography of the agent. This notion also helped inspire the series of successful novels by Charlie Higson that describe Bond's adventures as a youth.

Higson introduces his character in the novel *Silverfin* (2005) as a junior boy starting at public school. He is already, in appearance, a figure that fans of the older Bond would have no trouble in recognising. He is tall for his years, slender and with pale, grey-blue eyes and black hair. This he has tried to brush neatly off his forehead but one lock persists in falling over his right eye in a 'black comma'.

Bond did not fit the image of a gawky adolescent – bumptious and surly in manner, slovenly in appearance, inane in conversation and lacking in social skills. Instead of pimples and braces on his teeth, readers of John Pearson's biography of Bond are introduced to a young man of implausible maturity, both physical and mental. He already looks much as he will at the time of the adult stories, possessing the same strength, assurance and world-weariness. In his mid-teens he is already killing people, making love to sophisticated women and hurtling around the roads of Europe in his trademark Bentley which, fans are aware, he had acquired as early as 1933. We are asked to believe that although he was not yet 17 at the time of one adventure, he in fact looked 'a handsome 25'.

Although Pearson's book is skilfully written and exciting, somehow a Bond who had known shyness, early failure and rejection in love would have been far more interesting as well as more sympathetic. His constant and predictable success in all situations robs the character of a depth he could otherwise have had.

Realms of fantasy
In reality a rather ineffective agent

It goes without saying that the James Bond character, whether in the novels or on the screen, requires a considerable suspension of reality on the part of the reader or audience to be truly believable. It is not only that he displays a totally implausible range of skills and enough good luck for six people, but that hardly anything about his appearance or habits would make for an effective British secret agent. Let us consider the facts.

First of all, Bond is far too conspicuous. Someone who looks like – and has the presence of – a movie star would be noticed at once, and followed out of sheer curiosity. His too-perfect features would be remembered and the distinctive facial scar he has in the novels would make identification even easier for his opponents. Moreover, his furtive manner would be a further giveaway; hotel staff, taxi drivers and barmen would assume he was a spy even if he wasn't. His cover would be quickly blown, his opponents finding his lack of discretion laughably unprofessional.

Quite apart from his face, his clothing would give him away. Immaculately dressed, his tailoring would mark him out instantly as being not only British but reasonably wealthy, and every pickpocket and trickster in town would view him as fair game. In *From Russia With Love* Sean Connery walks about an Istanbul bazaar dressed in a Savile Row suit; surely it would be obvious at a glance that London had 'sent someone' to the region, and he would make an easy target for enemies to tail. Even the character's penchant for slip-on shoes would be a disadvantage. Every time he lashed out at someone with a karate kick his shoe would

fly off, and he would suffer the humiliation of having to hop around afterwards looking for it.

Finally there is the matter of his tastes in food and drink. Bond's expense account derives from the realms of fantasy and certainly not from any Whitehall department. In reality a British agent would have been issued with cash – probably in a brown envelope with a window – calculated to barely cover modest food and transport requirements. A single one of Bond's gourmet meals would wipe out the whole amount, and the agent would spend the rest of his mission living on limited means. If he were dining with others such as Vesper Lynd in *Casino Royale*, he would almost certainly have to pretend he wasn't hungry, and scan the menu for the cheapest items. As for the innumerable martinis, he surely didn't expect the British taxpayer to stump up for those?

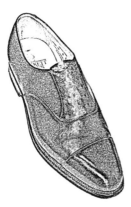

Superman?
Probably not ...

Bond is depicted, especially in the movies, in a constant state of mental and physical alertness. We must ask ourselves, is this state of affairs possible? The answer is most definitely not, especially taking into account Bond's age and lifestyle. Bond would have to be extremely fit to perform as he does, and could simply not consume tobacco or alcohol to the extent that Fleming's hero does. Anyone who sat up all night drinking and gambling would be hung over and exhausted until the following afternoon – a distinct advantage for his enemies if they were early risers. Smoking and drinking as the agent does, his eye would not be steady and neither, probably, would be his hands.

However effortless his physical prowess seems on screen, a great deal of his time would need to be spent practicing both judo and shooting. Only by constantly training his muscle-memory with hundreds of hours of routine could he achieve the stamina and the reflexes attributed to him. If he did not do this, his reactions would be too slow to deal with the extreme situations in which 007 finds himself. The novels also tell us that his nerves are jangled by his experiences. In real life a person in such a predicament would need considerable recuperation, and perhaps psychological counseling.

With regards to sex, his handlers would probably take significant steps to ensure there wasn't any, since this is notoriously the easiest way to be compromised. Pillow talk in which the agent mentioned his mission or his contacts could be picked up in a bugged room, and he could easily be overpowered or killed by intruders while in the throes of passion. Bond is supposedly about 35 years old; a man's physical fitness declines after 32, so he is already at a disadvantage, and sexually speaking he is about 20 years beyond the age at which male sexual drive reaches its peak.

In reality it is certainly possible for an agent to be as mentally and physically fit as Bond, but not if he lives the way Bond does. He could achieve the required prowess only by losing the entire social side of 007's lifestyle. His whole life would have to be given to routines of training. He could not have indulgent habits, and his diet would be strictly controlled. He could not afford the time to go out in the evenings. He could not have pastimes such as gambling that would distract his focus from his job, and he would be kept out of all unnecessary danger.

A valuable and well-trained asset such as Bond – an expensive, high-maintenance weapon – would be mollycoddled, protected, and nagged all the time by minders, coaches or other support staff. The Secret Service would not allow him to wander off and do as he liked; in fact a much more realistic notion of how such an operative would live is the case of Red Grant, Russian counter-intelligence agency SMERSH's chief executioner in *On Her Majesty's Secret Service*, who is brought out of seclusion only for missions.

MAKING BOND HUMAN
In sharp contrast to the constantly immaculate Bond portrayed by Roger Moore, Daniel Craig has played 007 as a more realistic figure, frequently out of breath, exhausted, disturbed and with disfiguring injuries that take days to heal.

At home with Bond
His residence in London

Bond's home is a rather anonymous place in which he lives alone and seems to do little more than recuperate between missions. Fans, however, have sought to identify its exact location. He occupies a flat in a 'plane-treed square off the King's Road, Chelsea' (*Moonraker*). John Pearson, in his fictional biography of Bond, identifies this as Wellington Square, a pleasant brick-and-stucco, late-Regency assemblage of terraced town houses built in about 1830. It is an archetypal English setting, like dozens of other anonymous squares in west London. It retains an atmosphere that is surprisingly quiet and discreet considering its proximity to the noise and bustle nearby. One side of the square is formed by the King's Road, and Sloane Square is no more than a few minutes' walk away.

Although he does not cook, Bond can order a meal with the confidence of an expert. In *Casino Royale* he explains to Vesper Lynd that he takes what he calls 'a ridiculous pleasure' in what he eats and drinks. This is in part because he is a bachelor. Since he does not do the cooking, he has no need to worry about what goes into the meals or how difficult it is to prepare, and he can be as choosy as he likes. He is also, because his training

has taught him to be observant and to take trouble over details, somewhat fussy. The main reason, of course, is that he takes the majority of his meals alone. It naturally makes solitary dining less of a chore if one is able to devise a balanced and imaginative meal. As a habitual smoker and drinker, it is actually unlikely that Bond's taste-buds are very acute when it comes to food. This is also why he favours sharp-tasting spirits and strong black coffee.

Action-fuelled lifestyle
Bond's plethora of leisure pursuits

For a busy man who is away from home so much, Bond somehow has time to maintain an enviable level of skill in a multitude of sporting activities and pastimes. Although his battleship-grey Continental Bentley is described in *Casino Royale* as 'his only personal hobby', Bond has a bewildering range of leisure interests, all of which he seems to pursue with noticeable ability.

He has a golf handicap that varies between six and nine, incidentally the same as Fleming's. In *Goldfinger* he plays at the 'Royal St Mark's' in Sandwich, Kent; the club exists, although it is actually called the Royal St George's. Bond was also an able skier in his youth, trained at the Hannes Schneider School in Austria (*On Her Majesty's Secret Service*) and, although he got out of practice in later life, he remembers enough techniques to escape down the mountainside at the end of the story.

In both novels and movies, Bond plays cards with legendary panache (*Casino Royale*), and is equally adept at underwater swimming (*Thunderball, For Your Eyes Only*). In the novel *Goldfinger*, he is sufficiently expert in unarmed combat to be writing a book about it. He has also been seen incidentally, in movies, fencing and riding with confidence. We cannot help but find ourselves wondering how Bond finds the time for this action-fuelled lifestyle?

Who'd have him?
Bond, the ultimate bachelor

Although one of the world's most famous bachelors, Bond has been married. In the novel and movie *On Her Majesty's Secret Service* he weds Tracy, the beautiful and headstrong daughter of mafia boss Marc-Ange Draco. The nuptials take place at the British Consul-General's office in Munich, Germany, but their happiness is, of course, short-lived: she is killed as they drive off on their honeymoon by Ernst Blofeld and his sidekick Irma Bunt. Although a deeply poignant incident, Bond fans would probably agree that it was for the best, since even a wife as spirited as Tracy would have hampered Bond's lifestyle and career.

On a second occasion, at the end of the novel and movie *You Only Live Twice*, he is apparently joined in wedlock (the ceremony is not described) by a Shinto priest to the diver Kissy Suzuki. Since he has, at the time, completely lost his memory and thinks he is a Japanese fisherman called Taro Todoroki, perhaps this one doesn't count. Although tender in his

dealings with Kissy, he seems to have no qualms about abandoning her to return to Europe once his memory starts to come back.

Perhaps James Bond is not such a catch as some of his female admirers might imagine. An article published in the 1970s suggested that Bond, although undoubtedly possessing appeal for women, would make a very unsatisfactory husband. As a long-time bachelor he would be set in his ways and reluctant to change. The novels make it clear that he is both a creature of habit and extremely fussy, especially where food is concerned. Any wife who cooked him a meal would doubtless be subjected to a torrent of detailed criticism regarding both the ingredients and the preparation.

He is also not wealthy, and the cost of a family would put a strain on his civil service salary. Unable to afford the trappings of luxury – his car and his hand-rolled cigarettes – he might well become resentful and difficult to live with. In addition he would be away from home a lot, and his spouse would spend a great deal of her time alone and worrying. To top it all, he would probably find it simply too difficult to curb his tendency toward philandering.

As for the sort of women he likes, he clearly has no particular preference for physical types, since he is happy to try his luck with women of all descriptions, and takes advantage of whatever situations his life and missions throw at him. He does, however, like married women best since paradoxically they present, to him at least, fewer 'complications'.

EVEN STUNTMEN HAVE NIGHTMARES!

*Bob Simmons, the stuntman who doubled for Sean Connery in **Dr No** and in several other movies, reported that the most terrifying moment of his career was when the poisonous spider that appears in the movie was placed on the pillow next to him.*

The man who made it happen
Broccoli's passion for the world of 007

Whatever the merits of Ian Fleming's Bond novels, his secret agent would never have reached a worldwide audience had he not become the hero of a series of movies, the most successful series of its kind in cinema history. This was overwhelmingly the achievement of one man, Albert 'Cubby' Broccoli, who not only brought Fleming's stories to the screen but, more than anyone else, chose the actors, the music, the locations and – once the scripts began to diverge from Fleming's originals – the plots.

Albert Romolo Broccoli (1909– 1996) was born in Queens, one of the Boroughs of Greater New York. 'Cubby', the nickname that would stick to him for the whole of his life, was acquired in childhood and was probably a reference to a character in a comic strip. His family, appropriately, was in the business of selling vegetables, and indeed he believed it was a relative of his who had first brought broccoli seeds to America in the 1870s. Although Cubby began life in the same profession as his father he quickly moved on to others, working for a time as manager for a firm of undertakers, before discovering the world of movies.

His cousin was an actor's agent in Los Angeles and when visiting him, Cubby decided to seek a future in that world. In 1940 he became an assistant director for Twentieth Century Fox on the Howard Hughes movie *The Outlaw*. No sooner had he begun to make a mark in Hollywood than America entered World War II and he found himself in the US Navy. His service there, however, was to be spent organising entertainments for the men, and thus allowed him to stay within show business. The rest of the entertainment industry, after all, was now also involved in the war, and he made many useful contacts during these years.

Once he resumed civilian life, Broccoli decided to become a producer. A man of a sunny and optimistic nature who inspired confidence in others, he formed a company, Warwick Productions, in partnership with fellow producer Irving Allen and relocated to London. However this enterprise failed on its first attempt at a movie and Cubby returned to California, where he became an actor's agent.

A few years later in 1951 he and Allen reformed Warwick Productions to make a wartime movie called *The Red Beret*. Movies about World War II were already a staple of cinemas on both sides of the Atlantic but the genre had not yet hit its stride, and the venture carried some risk. In the event, *The Red Beret* did extremely well in both Britain and the US, and Warwick Productions entered a period of conspicuous success that was to last for several years.

Its ship, however, struck a reef with the release of a movie that the two men had financed from their personal resources, *The Trials of Oscar Wilde*. Made in 1960, this was eight years before the decriminalisation of homosexuality in Britain and the subject was still an uncomfortable one; in the US even more so. There simply was not an audience for the movie, and as a result its producers went bankrupt.

This was the second time that Broccoli had reached a professional nadir, yet again he did not give up. He knew the novels of Ian Fleming, and confessed to having nurtured an ambition to film them. He subsequently made contact with businessman and producer Harry Salzman, who had bought the Bond movie rights, and persuaded him to go into partnership. They formed a new company, EON Productions Ltd, and set about raising funds.

In a visit to New York to meet the Head of United Artists, Arthur Krim, they took less than an hour to win the promise of $1 million to fund the filming of *Dr No*. This was

not a large amount, given the movie's potential disadvantages: the expense of flying cast and crew to Jamaica, and that there was no one in it who was an established star or a box-office draw. Nevertheless the gamble paid off, and it was to prove a worthwhile investment on the part of Krim.

The partnership lasted for 13 years and nine movies before Salzman, never as committed to the project as Broccoli, sold his share in EON to United Artists. Production continued regardless, with Cubby Broccoli as the sole producer and the movie *The Man With the Golden Gun* was released within a year.

Cubby continued in the role of producer until 1989, when his last movie was *Licence to Kill*. Although his health had begun to fail, he had managed to instil in other members of his family the same passion for the world of 007. His daughter Barbara had become involved in production, and has since replaced him as producer. His stepson, Michael G. Wilson, who was originally an accountant and whose connection with EON was financial, stayed to become a director of several movies.

Cubby Broccoli lived out his later years in California, passing away in June 1996. Surviving two serious professional setbacks, he had taken up the Bond genre and put it in an unassailable position as one of the most lucrative movie franchises ever.

BROCCOLI'S PRIVATE JOKE

Cubby Broccoli made reference to his past job at an undertakers by ensuring that in every Bond movie there was a coffin, or at least a mention of one. Intriguingly, Sean Connery had also had experience with them; one of the casual jobs he did during his youth in Edinburgh was polishing coffins.

Location, location, location
'We can't have him going to Blackpool'

The novels and movies were set in locations as prosaic as rural Kent and the Bank of England, and as exotic as Hong Kong and Rio de Janeiro. For his novels, Fleming placed much emphasis on locations he liked – Jamaica, New York, the Alps. The makers of the early movies were initially content with these, but looked increasingly further afield as audience sophistication and expectations rose. Once the age of mass air travel had begun, viewers ceased to be impressed by the mere fact that Bond could fly round the world with ease. Settings had to become ever more spectacular and producers had to try increasingly hard to overwhelm.

No one has ever pretended that a viable Bond movie could be made in Clacton, Manchester or Inverness. As one of those involved in planning the movies put it, 'We can't have him going to Blackpool.' Bond's time in Britain is spent either in the West End of London or in agreeable parts of south-east England. When he goes abroad it is only to the playgrounds of the rich, because his opponents are men of great wealth and they, too, would not think of spending their time in Blackpool.

Like Fleming, Bond has a penchant for the West Indies, or at least for the island of Jamaica. At the time the novels were written it was – more than any other place in the region – a resort of the well-heeled of Britain and the US. Fleming's connection with Jamaica was a matter of leisure,

New York City

Bond's is one of work – he is assigned there to deal with crime in what was still a British possession. Jamaica became independent in 1962, the same year in which the movie *Dr No* was released, and much of the island – its capital Kingston, for instance – has since become a dangerous place. The Bahamas, of course, were the setting for *Thunderball*, although that other gem of the Atlantic, Bermuda, strangely did not feature in any of the Bond stories.

Bond, like his creator, is at home in the US. Fleming was often rude about the country and its ways, but it offers not only scenery and a human landscape of useful heroes and villains but the prospect that a US location will increase sales of both books and movies there. In Europe, Fleming's knowledge of France's roads and

wayside restaurants is put to good use, as is his love of the Alps. Istanbul, featured in *From Russia With Love* and *The World is Not Enough*, is perhaps his most inspired setting – highly unusual (virtually unvisited by British tourists at the time), very strategic and extremely credible as the setting for a Cold War showdown. Japan is also a welcome departure in *You Only Live Twice*. The observations Fleming makes on Japanese customs and attitudes are intriguing.

The movies, of course, began by remaining faithful to the locations of the novels. These ran out, and when searching for new ones there was little point repeating what had already been shown. Locales with the necessary visual impact – such as Rio harbour – were quite understandably made use of, especially when they included a visually spectacular carnival that could be worked into the plot. It would be madness not to use settings like Venice and Paris. India and Thailand are highly impressive, as are Croatia, Panama and southern Chile in more recent movies. It will be a hard task to keep coming up with locations that can match these.

Place of work
Where the adventures begin

In the novels of Fleming and others, Bond works in the fictional MI6 headquarters on the seventh floor of a drably anonymous nine-storey building overlooking London's Regent's Park. The office of his superior M, guarded by Miss Moneypenny, is on the ninth floor, as is the Communications Department. The shooting range where Bond practices with his Walther PPK is in the basement and in between is the canteen in which, while awaiting new assignments, he often has lunch. He shares an office and a secretary (Leolia Ponsonby, then Mary Goodnight) with the two other members of the 00 Section – 008 and 0011.

The early movies tended to show only interiors but since MI6 moved to an eye-catching new headquarters on the Thames, the building – with its signature green glass windows – has featured conspicuously in several scenes, as has the surrounding area, known as the South Bank. According to a British magazine, when the movie *The World is Not Enough* was first shown at a London cinema, the audience included a party of MI6 staff who had attended as an office outing. When, in the pre-credits sequence, the Department's unmistakable headquarters building is attacked and the famous green windows are shattered, they burst into wild cheering.

The MI6 Building, London

Inspired, but not obvious
Sean Connery, the right man for the job

Sean Connery (1930–) seems like an inspired choice for the role of James Bond, but at the time of casting the first movie, *Dr No*, his suitability was not so obvious. Born in 1930 and brought up in the Edinburgh district of Fountainbridge, Connery's background was solidly working class. His father was a lorry driver and his mother a cleaning lady. He himself was small until his teens, when he rapidly sprouted to an imposing 6ft 2in (1.9m). His full name was Thomas Sean Connery, and he remained Tommy or – in Scots – 'Tammy' to those who knew him. Only when his name began to appear in theatre cast lists would he decide to opt definitively for 'Sean'.

Growing up he held a series of jobs that included service in the Royal Navy, lorry driving, delivering milk and a stint as a lifeguard at a swimming pool. He also began modelling for life classes at Edinburgh College of Art. It was not just his height or features that made him stand out. He had begun bodybuilding under the tutelage of a former Mr Scotland, and achieved some success, competing in Mr Universe in the 1950s. With physical fitness and a striking natural presence, he was clearly going to make his mark in something. In fact, at one point he almost became a professional footballer.

Connery also began working backstage at Edinburgh's King's Theatre, and was interested enough in what was happening on stage to begin playing parts in the productions. While doing yet another job, in the print room of a newspaper, he spotted a notice in one edition announcing auditions for a production of *South Pacific* at a London theatre and decided to try his luck. He was cast, and in 1957 he went on to appear in his first movie, the forgettable *Hell Drivers*, a story about long-distance lorry drivers for which his own

experience in that world must ideally have suited him. In the following year he travelled to Spain for the making of another picture, *Action of the Tiger*, which was notable only in that it was on this project that he first worked with director Terence Young, the man who would shape the Bond movies over the years to come.

The first truly memorable movie in which Connery appeared was Walt Disney's 1959 production *Darby O'Gill and the Little People*, for which his Irish name alone would have qualified him. Although one critic famously sniffed that he was 'merely tall, dark and handsome', the movie brought him considerable public attention, as did television work on a production of *Anna Karenina* two years later. By the time the first of the Bond movies, *Dr No*, was about to be cast, he was thought by some to be a very strong candidate.

Connery himself did not expect to get the role. Whatever he could offer in animal magnetism, he lacked any element of sophistication. He spoke with a native Scots burr (and indeed has done so ever since) that lost him credibility as an upper class

Englishman. He was unrefined in manner and he had tattoos (one read 'Scotland for Ever' and the other, 'Mum and Dad') on his arms that might prove inconvenient for a movie that involved physical exposure. Bond's creator would have agreed with this assessment. Although Cubby Broccoli had decided he wanted to cast this actor, Connery was unlike anyone Fleming had known, and the Scot was a world away from the author's notion of 007.

FIRST CHOICE

Ian Fleming's first choice for an actor to play 007 was allegedly his friend David Niven (1910–1983). Although a seasoned actor and much loved by audiences, Niven bore no resemblance to the description of Bond (who would somehow be unthinkable with a moustache, just as Niven would be difficult to imagine with a comma of black hair). He had also appeared in so many social comedy movies that he lacked any sinister element and was associated in the public mind with light humour or chaste and high-minded romance. He might thus have had too hard a task establishing credibility as a blunt and ruthless killer. He did, of course, appear to great effect as 007 in one Bond movie – the satirical 1967 movie **Casino Royale,** *in which he co-starred with Peter Sellers, Woody Allen and Ursula Andress.*

In the end Fleming allowed a woman to decide the actor's fate. He famously invited the young Connery to lunch at the Savoy. Among the guests was the author's friend Janet, Marchioness of Milford Haven, who afterwards told him that from a female perspective the Scotsman was all that viewers could desire. Fleming respected her judgement, and withdrew his reservations. Connery was perhaps as surprised as Fleming to find that actor and author got on well, and each discovered that the other was amusing company.

Fleming was fully won over after seeing *Dr No* on the screen, admitting that were he to write the books again his character would be more like Connery. He made a minor adjustment to Bond in a later novel that helped fit him more closely with the version of 007 the public had

come to know: in 1964 when writing *You Only Live Twice*, he revealed (in an obituary written by M) that the agent was half Scottish, the son of an engineer from Glencoe in Argyllshire.

Connery's lack of sophistication was gradually overcome under the tutelage of Terence Young, who had the actor work assiduously on social graces to learn the thousand nuances of gesture, movement and voice that would make him believable as a gentleman. This, together with Connery's natural on-screen presence and flair for action, produced a highly satisfactory result. Connery undoubtedly reaped rewards from his years as 007, in terms of both fame and fortune. However his own personality was so different to that of the agent that he became weary of constant association with him. In 1968 he gave up the role and looked for an acting career that would offer more variety. He came to see the Bond label as a hindrance.

Although he went on to star in many great movies Connery obviously retained some affection for 007 for in 1983, by now 53 and wearing a toupee, he agreed to return to the screen in the role. The movie was, of course, Kevin McClory's remake of *Thunderball*: *Never Say Never Again* (a title thought up by Connery's wife Michelle). The movie – and its star – was visually impressive but fans felt it did not match the work of EON Productions – *Never Say Never Again* had been made by an independent production company called PSO International. Because this was the only movie for which McClory had any claim on rights there was no question of further, similar productions being made by this company. *Never Say Never Again* remains an anomaly regarded, along with the unfortunate 1967 *Casino Royale*, as an illegitimate use of the brand, always to be classified separately from the rest.

NOT IN SYMPATHY
At the time he was cast, Sean Connery had read only two of Fleming's novels and said he felt no sense of empathy with 007, commenting at the time that he would not like Bond if he met him in the street. That is, of course, not surprising. Who, after all, would take much of a liking to a cruel looking, tough and taciturn man whose selfish and ruthless nature would have been apparent after a few moments of conversation? Bond is not supposed to be likeable but to be an effective weapon against the enemies of Britain. Whatever Connery thought of the character he played, he was able to re-model him to some extent in his own image. He succeeded in bringing a warmth and humour into his screen performances that were not obvious in Fleming's original novels.

Hard act to follow
The arrogant George Lazenby

When Sean Connery announced in 1968 that he had had enough of playing 007, an urgent hunt began for his replacement. This was already one of the world's plum acting jobs and, although it would naturally be difficult for anyone to follow Connery in a role he had made so much his own, competition would be fierce. While young men dreamed of winning the part, the producers were just as avidly trying to help them get it. Whoever was to be the new Bond, there must be time to introduce him to the public, get the media behind him, and make the next movie, *On Her Majesty's Secret Service,* which was due to be released in 1969.

George Lazenby (1939–) had arrived in London four years earlier from his native Australia. Born in

New South Wales, he had become a car salesman there and had proved himself extremely good at it. He had an unstoppable charm that enabled him – by his own account – to break sales records and to earn large commissions, which he spent on leading a somewhat Bond-like existence of champagne and fast cars. Searching for wider recognition,

he shipped to London and started from scratch in the car-sales business there, with the same success he had enjoyed at home. He also drifted into the world of male modelling and, with his chiselled features and wry smile, became both sought-after and amply rewarded – it is even claimed that he became the most highly paid male model in Europe at the time. He famously appeared in a television commercial for Fry's Chocolate and, although his name was not of course given, this made his face familiar to British viewers.

Lazenby was used to getting what he wanted, and he wanted very badly to be the next James Bond. His agent Maggie Smith, impressed by his arrogance, believed he could talk his way into the job. He subsequently began relentlessly to position himself for the part; buying a Rolex watch and a suit that had been made for Connery, and being seen driving an Aston Martin. He had sat next to Cubby Broccoli in a Mayfair barber's shop – almost certainly by deliberate subterfuge – and apparently impressed the producer as a potential 007, although it is possible that he lobbied both loud and long while the other man sat helpless in his chair.

Whatever the circumstances, Lazenby did well at audition. He performed at interview with trademark confidence; when asked 'How's your body?', he answered that it was better than Connery's. He screen tested impressively, and clinched the part by throwing himself with such gusto into a staged knife fight that he broke the nose of a stunt man. He won the part in competition against over 400 candidates, most of whom had far more acting experience than he had.

He was, of course, cast with outstanding actors in the movie *On Her Majesty's Secret Service* – Bernard Lee, Telly Savalas and Diana Rigg. He might well have come across as gauche and wooden, but in fact he delivered his lines competently enough, moved well on screen and looked very much the part. He also impressed audiences when, at the end of the movie, he had to handle the difficult emotional scene following the death of Bond's wife, Tracy.

Nevertheless the press leaped on rumours that he was proving difficult

(his self-importance had already become apparent in interviews) and that he and Rigg had a frosty professional relationship. Following a light-hearted remark of hers, it was widely reported that she deliberately ate garlic before their love scenes. It is not difficult to imagine that to Rigg, a trained professional who had attained stardom after years of work and discipline, a cocksure individual who 'outranked' her in terms of exposure yet lacked any useful experience or sense of deference may well have been hard to put up with. And any movie set is likely to be a battleground of egos.

On Her Majesty's Secret Service has been generally perceived as a weak Bond movie. It made less money than its predecessors, but this was partly because it was longer, and therefore could not be shown as often in cinemas during the course of a day. Lazenby was subsequently dismissed as a lightweight by many fans, but at the time Broccoli was happy enough with his performance to offer him a contract for seven more Bond movies. There seemed to be no doubt that the producers believed a satisfactory new

007 had been discovered: the next movie was to be *Diamonds Are Forever*, and he was expected to be the star.

Lazenby, however, decided differently. Without doubt he enjoyed the trappings of stardom and the glamour that went with playing the part, but he assumed he could now have these whatever he did. Amazingly, his publicist persuaded him that the image of a louche secret agent was in any case outdated and that the genre had no future in a decade dominated by youth rebellion. He refused to sign the contract, announcing even before *On Her Majesty's Secret Service* was released that he would make no further 007 movies. Broccoli advised him to consider this position very carefully. After all, he had no background as an actor on which to build a further career. He had a reputation as difficult to work with, and walking away from one of the most coveted roles in cinema would suggest he was also unreliable, if not mad. Lazenby, however, had made up his mind. He did indeed walk away, and has regretted it ever since. Apart from occasional, and unmemorable,

appearances in television dramas he has not been seen on screen since his spell as Bond. He gamely attends 007 nostalgia events, a brief but periodic chance to relive the stardom that was his for so short a time.

As for *Diamonds Are Forever* (1971), United Artists paid Sean Connery a large salary for him to reprise his role as 007 for what he thought would be the last time.

IN RETROSPECT

History has been somewhat kinder to George Lazenby than critics were at the time. In recent years his movie, **On Her Majesty's Secret Service,** *has been assessed more objectively, and is now considered by many to be one of the strongest in the series. It has also been argued that with any Bond actor it takes more than one movie to establish him properly in the role. Cubby Broccoli believed that, if he had stuck to the series, Lazenby could have proved a very good Bond.*

Almost inevitable
Roger Moore, the longest serving Bond

By the time Roger Moore (1927–) was cast as James Bond on the big screen, he had already played almost every possible similar character on the small one. Born in south London in 1927, he was the son of a policeman. Although his background was 'ordinary', it was not as proletarian as that of Sean Connery. He attended grammar school and was briefly at Durham University. Called up for National Service, as were all young men of his generation, he became an officer in the Royal Army Service Corps. He also studied at RADA where he was a contemporary of the Canadian actress Lois Maxwell, who was to find fame as Miss Moneypenny in the Bond movies.

At the age of 18 in 1945 Moore himself had begun appearing, as an extra or in very small parts, in movies including *Caesar and Cleopatra*, and by the 1950s was also working in television. Blessed with a conventionally handsome appearance he was also, for some years, a model

Caesar and Cleopatra

and became a familiar figure on the covers of knitting patterns, gazing into the distance in a succession of jerseys and cardigans. In 1958 he was cast in the television series *Ivanhoe*, and adopted the role of action hero that would define him for the rest of his career. He followed this with work on the US-made *Maverick*, a story about a smooth and personable gambler – the Brett Maverick of the title. Moore was cast as Beau Maverick, a cousin who possessed even greater smoothness.

Roger Moore had everything that would make him a star in terms of looks, presence and experience. He was now simply waiting for a suitable vehicle to take him further. His big break was not long in coming. In 1962, the year after making *Maverick*, he was given the part of Simon Templar in television series *The Saint,* based on the famous stories authored by Leslie Charteris. Templar was a Bond-like figure who devoted his life to combating crime, and did so more effectively than the police. His character's nickname, 'The Saint' (which struck terror in the underworld), came from the fact that he was on the side of good against the ever-ubiquitous evil.

Moore played this role until the programme ceased to be made, seven years later. It made him an international star, fixing him indelibly in the public mind as a gentleman-sleuth and as a television equivalent of Sean Connery, whose Bond movies were, at the same time, carrying all before them at the cinema. Moore eventually became tired of a part that lasted all of 118 episodes. He branched into cinema with some success – *The Man Who Haunted Himself* – but remained typecast in the world of louche skulduggery and was signed up in the same

year, 1971, for *The Persuaders*, as a wealthy and idle crime fighter.

It had been rumoured that Moore had been offered the role of Bond before Connery but that contract-commitments on television series *The Saint* prevented him. Moore has denied this. Despite his qualifications, he did not expect to become James Bond: there simply was no vacancy for a 007 and Moore was, in any case, now too old. Bond is supposedly in his mid-30s and by the time Moore was approached by the producers he was in his 40s. However his age was obviously seen as no deterrent either at that time or later, and Moore would go on to become the oldest as well as the longest-serving actor to take on this physically demanding part. He was 45 when he began the role and would be 58 when he retired, seven movies later.

Since his retirement Moore has devoted a good deal of time to UNICEF, for which he is a Goodwill Ambassador. He discovered this cause while in India in 1983 filming *Octopussy*, and has served it so well that he received a knighthood in the year 2000.

PRE-UNION

Several Bond stalwarts worked together on-screen before their appearance in the 007 movies. 1962 saw not only the release of **Dr No** *but also of* **The Longest Day,** *an epic about the Normandy landings of 1944. Darryl F. Zanuck's movie was packed with stars – including John Wayne, Henry Fonda, Richard Burton and Robert Mitchum. Among the cast was Sean Connery, who played an Irish soldier named Private Flanagan. Gert Fröbe, soon to win international plaudits for his portrayal of the character Goldfinger, was cast as a bumptious German sergeant known as 'Kaffekanne' – or coffee pot. Another popular German character actor, Curt Jurgens, appeared in the more exalted role of General Gunther Blumentritt, the German Chief of Staff. Fifteen years later, Jurgens was to meet Bond (in the shape of Roger Moore) when he played the role of villain Karl Stromberg in the movie* **The Spy Who Loved Me.**

Played for laughs
Moore's unique approach

Roger Moore's approach to the role was very different when compared to his predecessors, Sean Connery and George Lazenby. For one thing, he relished the attention and publicity that went with the part. While Connery had become increasingly resentful of being associated with the character, Moore was happy to trade on it.

Although he lacked the physical toughness and magnetism of Connery and, again, lacked credibility as a sinister or ruthless figure, he instead brought humour – a constant flippancy that some found funny and others irritating. He gave little impression of being fazed by the threats he faced, whether these were to his own life or to the survival of the world, and he had a witticism for every occasion. A number of these were adlibbed by Moore himself rather than written into the script, although the dialogue writers at the time were milking even dangerous situations for humour. Many serious fans of the genre threw up their hands in despair, seeing what had been an exciting action series apparently reduced to the level of a comic strip.

It was not just the Bond figure at the time that caused disquiet; the supporting cast contained some surprises too. Characters like Jaws, played by the extraordinary Richard Kiel, were credible in a Bond movie – at least until they lost all menace and fell in love. The character of Sheriff Pepper played by Clinton James who, like Kiel, appeared in two movies, was seen as an absurdity and an embarrassment. During Moore's tenure as Bond, an audience might laugh at the leaden humour or applaud the cleverness

Richard Kiel

of stunts but it would not, as had earlier been the case, sit on the edge of its seats with acute tension.

This comparative trivialisation was seen as fitting for the mood of audiences of the time. It was, in Britain and in other parts of the world, a period of vicious terrorism and there was enough real violence on the television news to negate the need for realism at the cinema. Viewers, faced with an apparently unwinnable conflict in Northern Ireland amongst others across the globe, craved an escapist world in which good would decisively triumph, without obvious effort and without losing its sense of humour. The movies were also considered family, rather than adult, entertainment and the level of violence had to be commensurate with that.

Moore had a point when he observed that this could help make the movies saleable in all parts of the world. 'You've got to remember,' he said, 'that there are some countries where they even ban the *Tom and Jerry* cartoons for their violence. There is very little blood in the Bonds and we don't lay the violence on with a trowel. We fill the pictures up with a lot of jokes. That's what makes the violence acceptable.'

Moore's interpretation of the role of James Bond did not win the approval of everyone, provoking anger among die-hard fans who considered that this approach brought about a significant loss of quality and credibility. However it was a valid attempt to redefine the character in light of the period in which his movies were made. To the thousands of viewers who came of age during the Moore era of the 1970s, he is the genuine article and the others are aberrations.

Moore himself, despite having a RADA background and credentials in other movies, was seen by some critics as an actor without depth and was dubbed 'The Man With the Wooden Delivery'. His narrow range of expressions was often cited as evidence of a limited ability. He himself has always responded to such brickbats with a cheerful robustness. A man who has reaped such rewards in wealth and fame from a supposedly meagre talent can afford to be generous, and he has

joked that as Bond he had only three expressions: raising one eyebrow, raising the other, or crossing both when grabbed by the Jaws character.

CONNERY: BOND OR M?
For the 1983 re-make of **Thunderball** *– entitled* **Never Say Never Again** *– there was talk of casting Roger Moore as 007 and Sean Connery as M. Connery had by this time acquired the necessary physical gravitas for this new role, but chose to remain in his original.*

Short lived
Timothy Dalton – a successful, but fleeting, Bond

A classical actor more accustomed to Shakespeare than SPECTRE, Timothy Dalton (1946–) was a popular choice to play Bond and was enthusiastic to take on the role. Born in Wales, he was 40 when unveiled as the new 007 for *The Living Daylights*, which was to be released in 1987. If Roger Moore had earned derision as a lightweight actor, Dalton was the exact opposite.

Classically trained and with a background in repertory, he was the first 'serious' member of the acting profession to take on the role of 007.

Entirely at home on stage, he had also worked extensively on screen, making his name in a succession of landmark historical productions that included *The Lion in Winter* (1968), *Cromwell* (1970) and *Mary, Queen of Scots* (1971). He had followed these with a spell at the Royal Shakespeare Company, acting in many of the major classics, and with television work in the US that made his face familiar to that audience. Dalton, for whom the adjective 'brooding' might have been specially coined, gave seminal performances as two of the most romantic characters in the canon of literature – Heathcliff in the movie *Wuthering Heights* and Mr Rochester in the BBC television adaptation of *Jane Eyre*. He was, quite simply, made for that sphere.

Dalton had apparently

been approached to play 007 in the wake of Sean Connery's departure, but declined the part – however tempting the financial rewards must have seemed – on the grounds that at 22 he was far too young. Physically he had much to recommend him. He was the right height (6ft 2in) and had black hair. He was known to be professional in outlook, easy to work with (qualities that had not always been found on a 007 set), and was keen to take the role not, as Lazenby had put it, 'for broads and bread' but because he relished the challenge of doing something different.

Dalton eventually accepted the role as the next James Bond after initially declining due to theatre commitments.

The Royal Shakespeare Company

He signed a contract for three Bond movies, but in the end made only two: *The Living Daylights* (1987) and *Licence to Kill* (1989). After the latter, studio litigation held up further Bond movies for a period of six years and by the time 007 was back on the screen, Dalton – a busy man with many projects to choose between – had taken other work.

Patience rewarded
Pierce Brosnan gets another chance

Pierce Brosnan is a native of Ireland. He was born in Navan, County Meath, in 1953 but moved to England 11 years later when his mother settled in south-west London. That same year, 1964, he saw a Bond movie – *Goldfinger* – and decided to become an actor. He trained at the Drama Centre in London.

Brosnan had the physical attributes to pursue a career in movies or television, and it was the latter that initially captured him. He was signed by the US NBC network to star in the popular television series *Remington Steele* about a firm of private investigators. In this he played a charming reformed criminal. Whatever this role brought him in terms of recognition, it was to prove a straitjacket when a job he badly wanted – that of James Bond – became available.

Bond producers EON Productions were interested in him and he was sent a script for *The Living Daylights*. However his NBC contract committed him to seven years' work beginning in 1982 and the movie was due for release in 1987. NBC cancelled *Remington Steele* after only four seasons, freeing him to take the part, but then considered whether to resume filming the series, doubtless realising that it would do no harm to their own viewing figures if a Bond actor were on board. In the meantime EON expected exclusive commitment and wanted him to work only for them or NBC. After much deliberation, NBC decided to film the new series; however, after making only four episodes, finally cancelled it altogether. Brosnan was at last completely free, but the ship had already sailed and he had lost the Bond role, which had been passed by default to Timothy Dalton.

Yet fate was to give Brosnan another chance. With Dalton impatient to move on to other things after just two movies, the role of Bond seemed tantalisingly within reach again after all. This time Brosnan was signed up, and made his debut in *GoldenEye* (1995), going on to appear in *Tomorrow Never Dies* (1997), *The World is Not Enough* (1999) and *Die Another Day* (2002). Brosnan's Bond had more in common with Roger Moore than Timothy Dalton. He was breezy, more given to quips and less to introspection. Brosnan had a very powerful screen presence and was perhaps, arguably, the most attractive actor to play the role since Connery.

Rugged and realistic
Daniel Craig, a new departure

Daniel Craig (1968–) is English. He was born in Chester and grew up in the pubs of which his father was landlord. He joined the National Youth Theatre at 16 years of age, and after grammar school went on to the Guildhall School of Music and Drama in London to train for a career on the boards. Graduating in 1991, he had a spell acting at the Royal National Theatre, and appeared in a series of movies.

As Bond, he proved an extremely controversial choice. He undoubtedly has strong charisma and a very powerful face that is dominated by a steel-trap jaw and eyes of a quite uncanny piercing blue. Yet it must be admitted that he looks more like a nightclub bouncer than a gentleman spy ('He's so UGLY!' exclaimed one venerable actor). He is unarguably less handsome than his predecessors, and despite the usual West End tailoring he looks much less sophisticated, seeming both inappropriate and ill at ease in a dinner jacket.

Whatever convention has to say about the character's wardrobe, Craig wanted to develop the role for himself without reference to those who had preceded him as Bond. He took as a starting point not the fact that Bond is a connoisseur of gracious living but that he is a trained assassin, with all the emotional numbness – or sheer nastiness – that such a person is bound to have. He wanted, he said, to explore the dark side of Bond's nature and in doing so he has won praise for his performances, not least from those who feel that the character is again becoming recognisable as Fleming's creation. Internet critics who greeted his initial selection with outrage and threatened to desert the cinemas have been largely silenced by the quality of his performances.

Craig is assisted in his reinterpretation by a more robust approach to direction and make-up. The fights in which he gets involved actually look like fights rather than exercises in choreography. He really looks as if he is getting hurt, he receives vicious-looking injuries and they remain visible for several scenes afterward. This is the first time, in other words, that the world of 007 is depicted not as escapist fantasy but as the dangerous place it actually is. There is as much chance of disfigurement and disability here as there is of a clean death from a perfectly aimed bullet.

Craig would have appeared already in a third Bond movie – the 23rd since the series began – had the current producers MGM not had financial difficulties. The movie *Skyfall* is now, however, due for release in November 2012. One wonders how long Daniel Craig's reign over the 00 Department will last, and who will succeed him? It is highly possible that promising candidates are already being scouted in the pages of *Spotlight*. Perhaps, somewhere, a small boy will be taken to see his first Bond movie – *Skyfall* – and is conceiving the ambition to become an actor…

Daniel Craig

The Bond girls
Beyond the beauty…

M uch of the appeal for Bond films relies upon the feature of beautiful women. In the novels, female characters have backgrounds and personalities as unusual as their names, and the movie heroines are just as interesting. Like the villains, the women are glamorous and cosmopolitan and they must not be too young or old; in their 20s is ideal, according to Broccoli. Bond, by convention, is never in love with these women, although they tend to lose their hearts to him. The Bond girls' role can vary from being a victim to a villain, or simply a beautiful and tempting love interest. Although often spirited women, traditionally they tend to be more decorative than functional, but in keeping with changing expectations they have become more proactive, intelligent and less passive – a trend that began with Barbara Bach's performance as Anya Amasova in *The Spy Who Loved Me*. Now, it is not surprising to see a Bond girl as 007's ally helping him to successfully complete his mission.

For the actresses, appearing in a Bond film can be a blessing or a curse. It gives them wide exposure, but often typecasts them. However, as the Bond films have evolved, many actresses – Terri Hatcher, Halle Berry, Famke Janssen to name a few – have had successful post-Bond careers.

So who are these Bond girls and the actresses who play them?

FILM	BOND GIRL	ACTRESS
Dr. No (1962)	Honey Rider	Ursula Andress
	Sylvia Trench	Eunice Gayson
	Miss Taro	Zena Marshall
From Russia with Love (1963)	Tatiana Romanova	Daniela Bianchi
	Sylvia Trench	Eunice Gayson
Goldfinger (1964)	Pussy Galore	Honor Blackman
	Jill Masterton	Shirley Eaton
	Tilly Masterton	Tania Mallet
	Dink	Margaret Nolan
	Bonita	Nadja Regin
Thunderball (1965)	Domino Derval	Claudine Auger
	Fiona Volpe	Luciana Paluzzi
	Patricia Fearing	Molly Peters
	Paula Caplan	Martine Beswick
	Mlle. La Porte	Maryse Mitsouko
You Only Live Twice (1967)	Kissy Suzuki	Mie Hama
	Aki	Akiko Wakabayashi
	Ling	Tsai Chin
	Helga Brandt	Karin Dor

FILM	BOND GIRL	ACTRESS
Casino Royale (1967)	Vesper Lynd	Ursula Andress
	Miss Goodthighs	Jacqueline Bisset
	Miss Moneypenny	Barbara Bouchet
	Agent Mimi/Lady Fiona McTarry	Deborah Kerr
	The Detainer	Daliah Lavi
	Mata Bond	Joanna Pettet
	Buttercup	Angela Scoular
On Her Majesty's Secret Service (1969)	Teresa di Vicenzo	Diana Rigg
	Nancy	Catherine Schell
	Ruby Bartlett	Angela Scoular
Diamonds Are Forever (1971)	Tiffany Case	Jill St. John
	Marie	Denise Perrier
	Plenty O'Toole	Lana Wood
	Bambi	Trina Parks
	Thumper	Donna Garrett
Live and Let Die (1973)	Solitaire	Jane Seymour
	Rosie Carver	Gloria Hendry
	Miss Caruso	Madeline Smith

FILM	BOND GIRL	ACTRESS
The Man with the Golden Gun (1974)	Mary Goodnight	Britt Ekland
	Andrea Anders	Maud Adams
	Saida	Carmen Sautoy
	Chew Mee	Francoise Therry
The Spy Who Loved Me (1977)	Anywa Amasova	Barbara Bach
	Naomi	Caroline Munro
	Felicca	Olga Bisera
Moonraker (1979)	Holly Goodhead	Lois Chiles
	Corinne Dufour	Corinne Clery
	Manuela	Emily Bolton
For Your Eyes Only (1981)	Melina Havelock	Carole Bouquet
	Countess Lisl von Schlaf	Cassandra Harris
	Bibi Dahl	Lynn-Holly Johnson
Octopussy (1983)	Octopussy	Maud Adams
	Magda	Kristina Wayborn
	Penelope Smallbone	Michaela Clavell
	Bianca	Tina Hudson

FILM	BOND GIRL	ACTRESS
Never Say Never Again (1983)	Domino Petachi	Kim Basinger
	Fatima Blush	Barbara Carrera
	Patricia Fearing	Prunella Gee
	Nicole	Saskia Cohen Tanugi
A View to a Kill (1985)	Stacey Sutton	Tanya Roberts
	Kimberley Jones	Mary Stävin
	May Day	Grace Jones
	Pola Ivanova	Fiona Fullerton
	Jenny Flex	Alison Doody
	Pan Ho	Papillon Soo Soo
The Living Daylights (1987)	Kara Milovy	Maryam d'Abo
	Rosika Miklos	Julie T. Wallace
	Linda	Kell Tyler
	Rubavitch	Virginia Hey
Licence to Kill (1989)	Pam Bouvier	Carey Lowell
	Lupe Lamora	Talisa Soto
	Della Churchill	Priscilla Barnes
	Loti	Diana Lee-Hsu

FILM	BOND GIRL	ACTRESS
GoldenEye (1995)	Natalya Simonova	Izabella Scorupco
	Xenia Onatopp	Famke Janssen
	Caroline	Serena Gordon
	Irina	Minnie Driver
Tomorrow Never Dies (1997)	Wai Lin	Michelle Yeoh
	Paris Carver	Teri Hatcher
	Prof. Inga Bergstrøm	Cecilie Thomsen
The World Is Not Enough (1999)	Dr. Christmas Jones	Denise Richards
	Elektra King	Sophie Marceau
	Dr. Molly Warmflash	Serena Scott Thomas
	Giulietta da Vinci	Maria Grazia Cucinotta
Die Another Day (2002)	Giacinta "Jinx" Johnson	Halle Berry
	Verity	Madonna
	Miranda Frost	Rosamund Pike
	"Peaceful Fountains of Desire"	Rachel Grant
Casino Royale (2006)	Vesper Lynd	Eva Green
	Solange Dimitrios	Caterina Murino
	Valenka	Ivana Milicevic

FILM	BOND GIRL	ACTRESS
Quantum of Solace (2008)	Camille Montes	Olga Kurylenko
	Strawberry Fields	Gemma Arterton
Skyfall (2012)	Eve	Naomie Harris
	Sévérine	Bérénice Marlohe

If you say so...
Fleming's description of SMERSH

In his novels, Fleming used descriptions of life inside the Russian counter-intelligence agency SMERSH, and the British Secret Service, that the majority of his audience could not have verified. Indeed in a preface to *From Russia With Love* he stated confidently that a great deal of what he described in the book was entirely realistic and that SMERSH – an abbreviation of the Russian words *Smiert Spionam*, or 'Death to Spies' – still existed and numbered, as of the year 1956, about 40,000 operatives scattered throughout the Soviet Union and the world. He went on to say that a man called General Grubozaboyschikov ran the organisation – presumably M's opposite number – and that he was accurately portrayed by Fleming in the novel.

In addition, Fleming claimed to have provided a realistic picture of the setting for one of the story's most important scenes – the conference at which it is decided to make Bond the target of an operation. He wrote that the address he had given for the organisation's headquarters – No. 13, Stretenka Ulitsa, Moscow – was correct and that its conference room was just as he has presented it; he itemised the furniture, the carpet, the door padded for soundproofing and even the four pictures on the walls. The men he placed within it were apparently all actual secret service officials who met there, in real life, for discussions of the sort that appear in the novel.

Needless to say, no one was in a position to argue with Fleming's

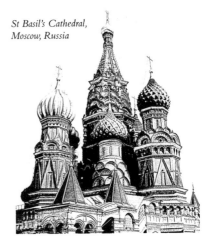

St Basil's Cathedral, Moscow, Russia

portrayal. Yet histories of Soviet intelligence, even those that were written after the Cold War, make no mention at all of General Grubozaboyshikov. One Western reader of the novel who travelled to Moscow took a photograph of the building on this site and sent it to Fleming who had stated that SMERSH headquarters was guarded by a pair of armed sentries, that pedestrians kept their eyes on the ground and that if they remembered in time they would cross the road to avoid the building altogether. In fact, the picture showed a row of unremarkable neighbourhood shops, of the old-fashioned kind that had sunblinds over their windows; there was not a gun-toting sentry in sight.

Fleming had already told readers in his novel *Casino Royale* that SMERSH ranked in the hierarchy of Soviet terror organisations above the notorious NKVD (the People's Commissariat of Internal Affairs, forerunner of the KGB) and was personally run by Lavrenti Beria (1899–1953), a man who definitely did exist and whose name to this day is synonymous with torture

and murder. Fleming stated that SMERSH was the most powerful and feared organisation in the USSR. Noting that it was thought never to have failed in a mission of vengeance, he claimed that it was believed to be responsible for the assassination of the former Bolshevik leader Leon Trotsky – a very real and spectacular coup for Soviet espionage – who was murdered while in exile in Mexico City in August 1940 (the assassin was in fact a member of the NKVD).

With so much information available, surely there could be no doubting the veracity of what Fleming wrote? Generations of readers and cinema-goers have indeed taken the existence of SMERSH for granted because it was featured so often and so authoritatively in the author's Bond stories.

True or false
Did SMERSH really exist?

The answer is yes, but it bore little resemblance to the body that Fleming used in his plots. The name was accurate; it was actually used, and it meant what Fleming claimed it did. The Soviet government was fond of such succinct abbreviations, and used them all the time to refer to organisations or departments. SMERSH, however did not exist at the time of Trotsky's death, nor was it operating in the mid-1950s when Fleming wrote his books.

The organisation was set up during a meeting chaired by Joseph Stalin in April 1943, when it was decided to restructure the parts of the NKVD that dealt with counter-intelligence within the armed forces. At that time the tide of war was beginning to turn in favour of the Russians and plans were made for the eventual reoccupation of Soviet territory lost in the earlier German advance. It was proposed that a department be created within the NKVD for the task of rooting out enemy agents, saboteurs and above all collaborators there. The suggested name for this was that of a much-used wartime slogan: *Smert Nemetskim Spionam*, or 'Death to German Spies'. Stalin, on hearing this, replied: 'Why should we be speaking only of German spies? Aren't other intelligence services working against our country? Let's call it *Smert Spionam* – SMERSH for short.'

The organisation quickly established a reputation for zeal, and Stalin valued it so highly that he removed it from the NKVD and put it under his direct control. Despite the purpose implied in its name, SMERSH did not hunt for foreign agents as Fleming suggested. Its task instead was, as originally

Joseph Stalin

conceived, to run a host of informers within the Soviet Army that would seek out the defeatist, the cowardly and the critical. SMERSH brutally discouraged any notions of nationalism or independence in the territories that would henceforth fall within the Russian sphere of influence, and was to be active in tightening Soviet control over these lands. In addition, all Soviet citizens (numbering some five million in all) returning from Germany – freed prisoners of war, former forced labourers and those who had simply fought on German soil as members of the victorious Red Army – had to be investigated (or in many cases simply eliminated) in case they should prove a danger to the State.

The persecution, imprisonment and murder of so many Soviet citizens was one of the darkest chapters in the history of communist Russia, and SMERSH was undoubtedly responsible for much of this reign of terror. It was, in other words, as terrible an organisation as Fleming suggested, although not for the reasons he gave. With a somewhat uneasy peace settling on Eastern Europe after World War II, its

objective was largely accomplished and it was disbanded in March 1946, its responsibilities passed on to the MVD (Ministry of Internal Affairs, the new name for the NKVD).

BOND AT THE WHITE HOUSE?

The biggest boost to Fleming's sales came when President John F. Kennedy listed **From Russia With Love** *as one of his ten favourite books. His brother Robert, who was at the forefront of the Cold War as Attorney General during the Cuban missile crisis, was also a fan of the novels, as were several of the Kennedy family sisters.*

From Russia with outrage
Bond viewed from behind the Iron Curtain

Pravda, the official Soviet newspaper at the time, was predictably scathing in its view of the Bond cult. An article written by journalist Yuri Zhukov in 1965, explaining that Bond's function

was to guard the interests of the propertied class, sneered that 007 inhabits a world where violence and aggression are seen as virtues, laws are created at the point of a gun, coercion and rape are regarded as bravery – or essential techniques – and murder is amusing.

As for 007's enemies, who are not only bested but humiliated with (from a Russian viewpoint) depressing regularity, the newspaper was at pains to point out that they were crude exaggerations. Describing these so-called caricatures as 'sham agents' of Soviet counter-intelligence, the writer went on to explain

that Fleming projected his own hatreds onto his fictional character, having him kill not only Russians but 'reds' and 'yellows'. As well as a persecutor of Soviet citizens, Fleming was cast in the article as a throwback to Nazi racialists and their theories, bent on destroying what he saw as 'impure races.'

Having proved this to his own satisfaction, Zhukov then claimed that Bond was merely a reincarnation of the youths that Hitler had trained to kill without conscience and he saw the movies as intended to mentally prepare young Americans to wreak destruction in South-East Asia with a similar mindset. Although Fleming himself was now dead, Bond was to be kept alive in the West because he taught those sent to kill in Vietnam, the Congo, the Dominican Republic and other parts of the world.

Surmising that Fleming had been further inspired by President Kennedy (assassinated almost two years earlier), who had expressed enjoyment of the novels and thus boosted their popularity, the article stated that the author had had the seal of approval from the 'mighty forces of reaction'. Zhukov ended his article with a swipe at the cast and crew of the cinema versions, implying that those who permitted their talents to be used in the movies had been dupes – or willing accessories – in furthering the reprehensible aims of Western capitalism.

Ironically, similar criticisms were voiced in the West by those who disapproved of the cynicism and violence in the stories. The reference to Vietnam is ironic. Zhukov's article appeared in *Pravda* in September 1965. By that time the novels had all been written, Fleming was long gone and three of the movies had already appeared; moreover in that year US involvement in Vietnam had scarcely begun.

HEROES EATING RICE PUDDING

Appearing on the television programme **Right of Reply,** *Fleming responded to criticism that his books contained too much sex and violence by remarking that one could not have thrilling heroes eating rice pudding.*

Quaintly old-fashioned
Fleming's novels are of their time

For all their sophistication, the Bond novels display an amusing bewilderment with things that are commonplace today. For example, the novel *For Your Eyes Only* describes 007's encounter with pesto during a dinner in Rome. Bond orders Tagliatelli Verdi and with it comes a Genoese sauce that, his companion explains, is 'improbably' concocted from basil, garlic and fir cones.

In another novel, Bond's incomprehension is shown when he is entirely bewildered by the ability of Auric Goldfinger's Korean manservant to smash heavy wooden banisters, and equally solid mantelpieces, with his hands and feet. Bond is asked if he has ever heard of karate; he replies that he has not. Goldfinger then explains that Oddjob is one of only three men in the world who have attained the black belt in this martial art, adding helpfully that karate is a branch of judo.

This enlightenment is necessary in spite of the fact that at the time Bond – supposedly an expert on these matters – is writing a manual entitled *Stay Alive!* in which he lists all the methods of unarmed combat known to the secret services of the world.

Sometimes Bond is merely quaint. He lives in a society that has not yet become 'multicultural' in the modern sense, and yet the criminals he must pursue can come from any racial background. This is shown when, discussing the hoodlums of Harlem and Jamaica with whom he will tangle in the novel *Live And Let Die*, he makes some rather quaint observations about their attitudes to law and drinking habits.

THE LEGACY WILL FOREVER REMAIN, BUT WILL BOND?

Bond has several times seemed too dated a concept to continue. EON Productions, which makes the movies, decided in 1981 that For Your Eyes Only would be the last. After consideration, however, they would have realised that action movies continue to make money and that there were still enough Bond fans of all ages to ensure the lasting popularity of the genre.

Ace of clubs
Upper-class trappings pervade

Bond has the tastes – and frequently the lifestyle – of the very rich without being one of them, and this is something his readers vicariously enjoy. His upper-class trappings are those of luxury and refinement, not of stifling etiquette and 'correct' behaviour. He himself is quietly amused by the conservative Establishment figures with whom he sometimes has to deal.

Blades, a fictitious club referred to in several of the novels, is situated in St James's Street and is probably modelled on Boodle's, to which Fleming belonged. M is a member, but Bond would probably consider it too stuffy for his taste. What some would view as a fixation with snobbish, old-fashioned institutions and attitudes pervades the Bond novels, which perfectly mirrored the views of their author and his circle.

Such places are, however, always incidental to the plot, and are used merely as background. 007 may be able to move easily in this world, dressing correctly, playing cards with skill and discussing vintage wines, but he quickly escapes from it as soon as a new assignment beckons. As for snobbery, many readers expected, and perhaps enjoyed it.

IT'S A SMALL WORLD…

Ken Adam, the production designer who created many of the spectacular Bond sets, was a wartime fighter pilot with the Royal Air Force. There is nothing unusual in that, except that he was born in Germany and had not, at that time, been naturalised. He was thus the only German to fly for the RAF's Fighter Command in World War II.

For her majesty's service
What awards has Bond received?

First is the CMG, or Companion of the Order of St Michael and St George. This award, first established in 1818, is almost exclusively presented to diplomats and those who have served the Commonwealth in some capacity. At the end of the novel *The Man With the Golden Gun* Bond is offered promotion within that Order to the rank of Knight Commander (KCMG), but declines to become 'Sir' James Bond instead because he dreads the notion of being a public figure.

As a veteran of World War II, Bond is also likely to have the Defence Medal, the 1939–45 Star, as well as the campaign star for any theatre in which he served. He has, apparently, two rows of medal ribbons; this implies that there are other medals. His Scottish housekeeper looks after this collection, polishing

them on the rare occasions that he needs to wear them, but he has no idea where she keeps them.

Not only appreciated by his own country, in the movie *A View to a Kill* Bond is awarded the Order of Lenin by the Russian government because the KGB is grateful to him for having eliminated their rogue agent, Zorin. John Gardner, author of several Bond novels and a biography of the agent, has Bond receive the same award in one of his novels, from President Gorbachev.

TOO MUCH FOR TOM!

John Barry was expected to write a theme song that included the title and made reference to the plot of the movie **Thunderball**. *He decided instead to compose one about the character of Bond, and called it 'Mister Kiss-Kiss-Bang-Bang', a nickname bestowed on 007 by an Italian journalist. It was recorded by Shirley Bassey, but shortly before the movie's release the distributors, United Artists, returned to their original demand for lyrics specific to its theme. Bassey's song was removed and another was written, in frantic*

haste, by Barry and Don Black. Because the theme song was usually interwoven, as incidental music, throughout the movie, the whole soundtrack had to be reworked and only about half of it was ready when **Thunderball** *appeared at cinemas. Tom Jones performed the new version. He recalled that, while singing it in a recording booth, he fainted. He closed his eyes on reaching the long, high, final note – and opened them to see the walls swimming.*

Tom Jones

Struck a chord
Barry synonymous with Bond

In 1961 the movie *Dr No* was in production, and the composer Monty Norman (1928–) had been hired to provide the music. He had written a score with which the producers were not happy and John Barry (1933–2011), a musician and composer from York, England, was therefore asked to do some additional work on it.

At the time he was a much less well-known composer than Norman, but he made a major contribution to the success of the movie. Norman was exclusively credited with providing the music because he was the one with whom a contract had been signed, but to this day it is not clear which man was responsible for composing the *James Bond Theme*, one of the most well-loved, evocative and instantly-recognisable snatches of music in the history of cinema.

Barry was not employed on the next Bond movie, *From Russia With Love*, because Lionel Bart – another better-known composer – had already been signed up. Once again,

however, Barry made a contribution. He and Bart worked well together, and would collaborate on the seminal movie *Zulu*. Barry in fact composed an alternative James Bond theme for *From Russia With Love* and it was to be reprised in later movies: *Thunderball, You Only Live Twice, Diamonds Are Forever* and *Moonraker*.

Barry's musical style was a rich blend of jazz and pop, using brass, electric guitar, synthesisers, bongos and xylophone. In mood it was very much in keeping with the then-current fashion for 'lounge music' – restful, tropical-style rhythms alternated with energetic rushes – bursts of exotic sound and the apparently loose, improvised quality of a jam session.

Barry's music perfectly fitted the time and came to seem the only appropriate style for the type of movie the Bond genre represented – tense, fast-paced, thoroughly modern and set in far-flung locations. Other composers began to imitate the soundtrack, just as other producers emulated the format. With his score for *Goldfinger*, Barry is considered to have brought to perfection the trademark Bond sound. He would maintain it, with constant modifications, for 11 movies until his final production, *The Living Daylights*.

Barry was the first composer to make use of synthesisers in a movie soundtrack. He would also use established stars to sing the themes, whether from the world of pop or from other branches of music. Who can forget Shirley Bassey singing the theme tune of *Goldfinger*? He composed not only the title music for the movie but wrote a host of incidental pieces, which gave a pleasant continuity to the productions.

After *The Living Daylights* health problems prevented Barry from working on a further movie, *Licence to Kill*, and he passed the baton

– literally – to another composer, David Arnold. Arnold had produced an album in 1997, *Shaken and Stirred*, which offered his own arrangements of the Bond music. Barry liked it enough to recommend the composer to Barbara Brocolli, and Arnold went on to score the later movies *The World is Not Enough, Die Another Day* and *Quantum of Solace*. Arnold is currently confirmed to score the latest Bond movie, *Skyfall*.

Appearance in High Court
Who wrote the James Bond Theme?

The controversy over who had actually written the *James Bond Theme* was to run a long time. Some 16 years after the theme was written, an article appeared in *The Sunday Times* in which it was stated that John Barry was the composer. Monty Norman, the official composer on the first Bond movie *Dr No* in which the music appeared, sued the paper and the case went to the High Court.

Barry appeared as a witness for the defence and recalled that, in return for a flat fee (as opposed to royalties), he had been asked to prepare some additional arrangements and add material to the score; while doing this he wrote the theme. However the jury did not accept that he was unambiguously the writer of the music in its final form, and found in favour of Norman.

Whatever the facts, it is indisputable that John Barry's name is more indelibly associated with the Bond movies than that of any other musician past or present.

Carly Simon

NOBODY DID IT BETTER

Of all the memorable music that accompanies the Bond movies, probably the most important – in terms of taking on a life of its own and becoming successful regardless of its origins – was the song **Nobody Does it Better,** *composed by* **Marvin Hamlisch and sung by Carly Simon** *as the theme to the movie* **The Spy Who Loved Me.**

Tested ingredients
The successful Bond formula

Long-standing Bond producer Cubby Broccoli once said that he was constantly looking for new ideas to put in the movies, and that as soon as one was completed he would be thinking about the next. However there are certain elements that were always included being, as they were, tried-and-tested ingredients of the popular Bond formula.

One key ingredient is that there must always be an exciting pre-title scene to grab audience attention. Another is that there must always be the collection of stock characters: beautiful girls and a villain of the affable and sophisticated variety, never personally thuggish as he has henchman to look menacing and to carry out the atrocities.

The settings must always be exotic enough to impress viewers, and at the end of each movie there must be humour as well as, for the movie's hero, a girl. It's a formula that clearly works and has been a long-standing favourite with audiences throughout the world.

PACE-SETTER
Scriptwriter Richard Maibaum adapted the novel From Russia With Love *for the screen and completed the script in a record six weeks, working without collaborators. 'The others have taken considerably longer,' he recalled, 'but it remains my favourite.'*

Giant leap
Why did Bond go into orbit?

When the first of the movies came out in 1962, the Space Race was a major international preoccupation, yet it would not be until 17 years later that a Bond movie enjoyed an extraterrestrial setting. *Moonraker* was the novel set in Kent, in the everyday surroundings of St Margaret's Bay. It was deemed too dated, and too prosaic, to bring to the screen in its original form and the title word – which has nothing to do with the planet and is actually an old term for a lunatic – gave the team an opportunity to introduce a space theme. 1977 was the height of the fixation with gadgetry in the cinema,

presenting the movie designers with a splendid opportunity to include some space age props and locations. With the settings for Bond's adventures becoming increasingly, eye-poppingly exotic, each production had to outdo the last. Space provided a chance to do something entirely different. One of the more inane plots for a Bond film, *Moonraker* follows Bond as he trails the villain, Sir Hugo Drax, from California and Venice to Brazil, discovering that his opponent's objective is to destroy humanity with a deadly gas and then repopulate it with a master race, which he will rule from a space station. He owns a fleet of space-shuttles and Bond steals one of these to fly to Drax's headquarters. It is here, in orbit, that the final battle takes place between the two, accompanied by their henchmen.

JUMPING FROM NEW HEIGHTS

For the epic bungee jump in the movie **GoldenEye,** *performed as part of the movie's opening sequence, stuntman Wayne Michaels plunged 640ft (195m), setting a new world record. He jumped from the*

Verzasca (also called the Contra) Dam in Switzerland, near the city of Locarno. At 720ft (220m) high, it is famous through its connection with **GoldenEye,** *and is in fact considered the most well-known bungee jump in the world. In fact, it has become something of a thrill for the more adventurous Bond fan to try.*

Verzasca Dam, Switzerland

M for mystery
Bond's superior

M, the head of the British Secret Service in the Bond stories, is an enigmatic presence in the first Bond novels, and only incidentally do we learn more about him. He is revealed to be Admiral Sir Miles

Messervy, KCMG, a career naval officer who gave up the prospect of further promotion to enter the world of espionage. A bachelor, he lives near Windsor, belongs to the fictitious Blades Club in London's St James, paints wild orchids as a hobby, and never leaves the Home Counties. While in the later movies M pops up in all corners of the world for urgent consultations with 007, the character originally went no further afield than his fishing holidays in Hampshire.

The directors of Russian counter-intelligence agency SMERSH, planning a 'hit' against British MI6, decide in the novel *From Russia With Love* that M is not high profile enough to assassinate; because the public is unaware of his existence, his death would send no message to the British people. He would also be hard to kill, since SMERSH would prefer to deal with such

Windsor Castle

a target on neutral territory and M could not be lured abroad. To shoot him in a London street, they conclude, would not be refined.

Gradually, however, movie audiences became accustomed to seeing M in settings other than his office. One of the more implausible moments on screen comes at the end of *On Her Majesty's Secret Service* when, at Bond's wedding reception, M is seen chatting amiably with the bride's father, an international criminal. We subsequently discover that he has his own personal submarine – not exactly an essential for someone who so seldom goes anywhere. One can only imagine how quickly that would fall victim to Whitehall spending cuts!

M was memorably played in the early movies by veteran actor Bernard Lee – from *Dr No* in 1962 to *Moonraker* in 1979. Robert Brown then took over the role, and was replaced in 1995 by Judi Dench in *GoldenEye*. By this time the British public was accustomed to the notion of a female head of the Secret Service; Stella Rimington had been a very high-profile Director-General of MI5 since 1992, and it was felt that cinema audiences could make the necessary mental adjustment. The casting seems to have been a success for Dench, whose triumphs on stage and screen are too numerous to mention, has not only added further star-quality to the cast but has redefined the relationship between M and Bond to include an inter-sexual banter that audiences enjoy.

JUST KIDDING

Bond may show little sense of humour in the novels, but his creator was known for an engaging sense of self-mockery. In the novel **You Only Live Twice** *M's obituary of 007, appearing in* **The Times,** *describes how a series of popular novels had been produced about the agent, and states that if their quality or their degree of accuracy had been any greater the writer could have been liable to prosecution under the Official Secrets Act. It is, according*

to M, indicative of the disdain with which the Secret Service views the books that no legal action has, to date, been taken against either the author or the publishing company responsible for what he describes as high-flown and romanticised caricatures.

Stolen gold
A hijacked name

Erno Goldfinger (1902–1987), a highly controversial London-based architect, was infuriated to discover that one of Fleming's characters had been given his name. Goldfinger had, in fact, several characteristics that would have made him an effective villain in one of the stories. Hungarian born but having lived and worked in Paris before settling in London, he had the cosmopolitan background, and the foreign-sounding name and accent, that have always been almost *de rigueur* for 007's opponents. Furthermore he was considered to be a man of an imperious nature as well as having a vicious bad temper, and to possess absolutely no sense of humour.

The modernist buildings he designed were generally unpopular, although time has in some cases increased the affection with which the public regard them. Goldfinger came to London with his wife in 1934 and among his first projects was his own home, Nos 1-3 Willow Walk in Hampstead. Then, as now, this was a picturesque and historic corner of London, and the erection of his large, ostentatiously-modern house (which ironically is now cared for by the National Trust) caused considerable disquiet, not least because older and more sympathetic buildings had to be demolished to make way for it. It is fascinating to learn that one of those who joined in the objections was Bond's creator, Ian Fleming.

Goldfinger increased his fame as the designer of several of the most conspicuous tower blocks. Perhaps his most durable work, the 31-storey Trellick Tower near Ladbroke Grove in west London, constructed between 1968 and 1972, has endeared itself to sections of public opinion and is listed as an architectural monument. Nevertheless Goldfinger, in his time, was associated in many minds with a type of architectural arrogance and ugliness.

Fleming had nurtured a dislike of Goldfinger since the architect had cleared the row of Hampstead cottages to create his new home. One day, more than 20 years after that incident, Fleming heard more about him from the cousin of Goldfinger's wife while playing golf. The personality, and the name, suggested someone straight out of a 007 novel and – rather in the way that the name 'Bond' supposedly came to Fleming out of the blue – Goldfinger must have struck him as perfect for a book title. It brought with it more than just plot ideas – the international traffic in gold, manipulation of the market, and the opportunities for crime that it presented. It also offered at least one location for the story, since the world's best-known gold deposits were at Fort Knox, Kentucky and this meant that there could be a US setting for the story.

The novel *Goldfinger* was published in 1959. Although the novel's villain was not an architect, did not live in Hampstead and had the Christian name Auric rather than Erno, there was an immediate threat of legal action against the publishers, Jonathan Cape, from the architect. Indeed, it was likely for a short while that the title would have to be changed. Fleming, unrepentant, suggested that every copy of the book should contain an erratum slip altering the villain's name to 'Goldprick'

– and explaining why! In any event, there was nothing in the story to suggest unambiguously that more than Goldfinger's name had been appropriated, and the architect was placated. Cape offered to pay his legal costs – as well as granting him six free copies of the novel.

Fleming must have enjoyed his revenge. The publication of the book, and the subsequent movie, made Goldfinger a household name throughout the world, but one that has ever since been associated with greed and criminality rather than great buildings.

'NO, MISTER BOND, I EXPECT YOU TO DIE!'

These lines spoken by German actor Gert Fröbe in Goldfinger had to be dubbed by a British actor, Michael Collins, because Fröbe could not speak a word of the English language.

Sincerest flattery
Bond spawns a new genre

The 1950s and 1960s were already an era of spy fiction, but Fleming brought glamour, high living, snob appeal and sensuousness to a world that had been characterised by a drab and gritty realism, replacing the crumpled trench coat that was the Cold War spy's badge of office with a dinner jacket. The movies and television shows of this period subsequently created a fashion for espionage stories that slavishly followed this new Bond formula, and the public could not get enough of them.

The Man from Uncle

The Man From Uncle was conceived in 1964 and ran as a television series, made by the NBC network, until 1968. Initially it had a single hero, an agent called Napoleon Solo played by Robert Vaughn, but the swift rise to popularity of his sidekick Ilya Kuriakin (played by Scottish actor David McCallum), resulted in the pair being cast as partners. Leo G. Carroll, a veteran character actor, played their boss – the 'M figure' – with suitable avuncularity.

Such was the association of suave agents with the UK in the wake of Bond that, even though *The Man From Uncle* was made by a US network, two of the three principal cast members were British, and the third one sounded as if he was. The worldwide appeal of the 'goodies' was however broadened by the fact that, rather than belonging to the Secret Service of any single country, they were members of a multi-national organisation, the fictional United Network Command for Law Enforcement (UNCLE). Unlike Bond, they did not take part in the Cold War; the only enemy they ever faced was an international criminal body and this, in the tradition that Fleming had already established, was known by the acronym THRUSH.

David McCallum

The meaning of the name was never explained to mystified viewers of the series, but for those who read one of the novels spawned by it, a translation was provided. The truth turned out to be so preposterous that perhaps we would have preferred not to know. THRUSH, it transpired, was an abbreviation of Technological Hierarchy for the Removal of Undesirables and the Subjugation of Humanity. This sounds so much like a branch of local government that one half-expects to hear they are also responsible for disposal of dog mess and garden refuse. One can only imagine the difficulties that fitting suitable words to these initials must have caused the unfortunate author.

The television producers of *The Man From Uncle* followed the Bond formula fairly closely, even though two heroes were involved rather than one. There was extensive use of gadgetry and the script was as loaded with flippant wisecracks as the 007 movies would be in the Roger Moore era. Indeed the series was to experience a sharp drop in ratings as it descended into trite humour at the expense of excitement. The two agents were frequently seen in dinner jackets, posed in a similar manner with pistols and shoulder holsters, and they clearly had the same level of sophistication as Fleming's hero in terms of wines, women and foreign countries – as well as the same hugely generous expense accounts.

There was also copious use of beautiful girls. One feature of such stories, inspired by Pussy Galore's flying circus of women pilots in the Bond story *Goldfinger*, was the deployment of private armies of female 'henchpersons', typically dressed in identical – and highly fashionable – catsuits or mini skirts, and often with white knee-high boots. Sex was not conspicuous in *The Man From Uncle.* In accordance with the mores of family entertainment and prime-time television, these agents did nothing more improper than 'snog' the girls at the end of each episode. In any event, the television series' stars Vaughn and McCallum rose to international fame as the men from UNCLE.

THE PROBLEM WITH NAPOLEON

Any resemblance between **The Man From Uncle** *and the Bond movies was far from coincidental. Norman Felton, the producer of the television series, admired Ian Fleming's work; when creating the plots and characters he had sent his material to Fleming and asked for advice. It was actually Fleming who came up with Napoleon Solo, the name for the central character played by Robert Vaughn, yet this at once caused problems. The television series was broadcast in the same year that* **Goldfinger** *was released and in the movie there was a villain with the name Solo. Although Fleming was happy for Felton to use it – he had after all given it to him – EON Productions, as makers of the*

Bond movies, threatened legal action if the name was used. The matter was eventually settled, and Napoleon Solo from **The Man From Uncle** *rapidly eclipsed his Bond namesake in recognition.*

Our Man Flint

The character Derek Flint, memorably played by James Coburn, was the eponymous hero of the movie *Our Man Flint*, made in 1966. By the time the movie was released, audiences knew exactly what to expect from the genre, and they were not disappointed. The agent's name was just as 'short and bland' as Bond's. The movie poster depicted the rangy Coburn clad in a tuxedo and sprawling in a state-of-the-art swivel chair. Clutching a pistol and a cocktail, he is surrounded by the usual images of leg and cleavage. Flint was an American who belonged to a body that must surely take the prize for the silliest acronym of the lot: ZOWIE (Zonal Organization for World Intelligence and Espionage). He enjoyed a lifestyle that even James Bond might have envied. No Scottish housekeeper for him; he shares his home with four young and nubile women who make his breakfast between them. His 'unique selling point' as an agent was that he could stop his heart at will and pretend to be dead – a trick that would naturally come in useful.

The script of this particular movie made no secret of its indebtedness to the Bond craze. It must be very difficult to make such a movie, for the producers walk a fine line between genuine excitement and parody. Indeed it proved impossible to keep the plot from becoming pastiche, and it was clearly easier simply to play it for laughs. Flint is offered gadgets for his mission that are directly inspired by Bond – an attaché case containing a throwing knife, and even a Walther PPK, 007's iconic weapon. His standby is a cigarette lighter that has 82 different functions, 'Eighty-three, if you wish to light a cigar!' as he quips. In a Marseilles restaurant, he causes a distraction by starting a fight with a British agent – 0008 – played by an actor who bears a noticeable resemblance to Sean Connery.

The Liquidator

Another Bond-like 'hero' of the time was the character Boysie Oakes in John Gardner's *The Liqiudator*, a movie released in that optimum year for spy movies, 1965. This story of a professional assassin was closely based on Gardner's novel, the first in a series of Oakes adventures that were penned by the man who would go on to become the most prolific author of James Bond stories to date: John Gardner wrote 16 novels, Ian Fleming 14.

The Liquidator was not a serious movie, as could be seen by a glance at the cast list. Two immensely popular actors, Eric Sykes and David Tomlinson – the former associated with television situation comedies, the latter with Walt Disney productions – ensured that the audience expected to laugh. Oakes himself, played by Rod Taylor, was an American, recruited through a misunderstanding into the British Secret Service as an assassin. Not wanting to lose the traditional millionaire's lifestyle that goes with spying (though only in the make-believe world of movies), Oakes hires a *real* killer

– a character played by Sykes – to carry out the dirty work for him.

A tongue-in-cheek look at Bond's world with a hero who, for once, is refreshingly vulnerable, *The Liquidator* is still worth watching today. During the opening credits it featured a memorable song by Shirley Bassey, who would later come to be associated with the Bond movies.

OH, BROTHER!

Sean Connery's brother Neil, a Scottish plasterer, was signed up to play a secret agent in the movie **Operation Kid Brother,** *an Italian production released in 1967 to cash in on Bond-mania. It proved to be his only venture into movies.*

Open to abuse
007 through the eyes of early satirists

Fleming's style, and the characteristics of his heroes and villains, lent themselves easily to parody, and as the books became international bestsellers they naturally attracted a noticeable degree of ridicule. Much of this was in magazine articles, but some take-offs were detailed enough to be published as books in their own right.

One of them was the *Harvard Lampoon's* parody novel *Alligator*, published in 1962, which makes waspish but affectionate fun of the genre. The *Lampoon*, founded in 1876 and regarded as the most famous college humour magazine in America, was known for razor-sharp mockery of literary forms (the short novel *Bored of the Rings* was to be another of its successes). The novel *Alligator* describes a plot by the international criminal organisation TOOTH to kidnap the British government, a scheme confounded by the agent J★mes B★nd. Holding up to ridicule the pithy, punchy titles favoured by Fleming, the book lists other novels supposedly in the series, including: *Toadstool, Lightningrod, Monsieur Butterfly, For Tomorrow We Live, Scuba Do – Or Die, Doctor Popacatapetl, The Chigro of the Narcissus* and *From Berlin, Your Obedient Servant*.

In the cult year of 1965, when Bond references appeared throughout the international media, a stone-age version of the agent – 'James Bond-rock' – even appeared in an episode of the cartoon *The Flintstones*. As regards outright parodies of the Bond adventures (as opposed to imitations of them) the US television series *Get Smart*, which ran from 1965 to 1970, was the most memorable. It took its title from the name of the lead character, Maxwell Smart (Don Adams), the incompetent 'Agent 86' whose bacon was always saved by his loyal female sidekick '99', played by Barbara Felton. Smart was always pitted against an organisation called KAOS, and naturally defeated them more by luck than design. His famous shoe phone was a nice satire on the Bond craze for gadgets.

The power of Powers
The Austin Powers *trilogy*

It is a tribute to the durability of Cubby Broccoli's work that, an entire generation later, spoofs were again being made and movie-goers of the 1990s and 2000s could easily understand the references. The three *Austin Powers* movies were produced between 1997 and 2002. Although

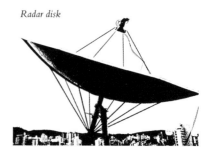

Radar disk

the character of Powers, played by Canadian Mike Myers who co-wrote the scripts, has none of James Bond's mannerisms, the movies are deliberately modelled on 007 epics of the Sean Connery era.

The first of them, 1997's *Austin Powers: International Man of Mystery*, introduces the character Dr Evil, a villain who is intent on holding the world to ransom, and who will be Powers' nemesis throughout the series. A 007 actor could have read the script for the first *Austin Powers* movie and found all the things he expected in terms of plot, action and gadgetry in Bond, without realising it was a spoof version. With the other Powers movies, 1999's *The Spy Who Shagged Me* and 2002's *Goldmember*, the Bond reference is obvious at once from the titles. Indeed MGM, distributor of the 007 movies, threatened legal action over the name of the latter, and it had for a short time to be removed from promotional material. Bond parody is in any case ubiquitous throughout, and probably led to greater interest in the original movies.

Besides Dr Evil, there is a henchman called Random Task whose name is directly lifted from Oddjob, and there are lines of dialogue whose inspiration is well known: 'Do you expect them to pay?'; 'No, I expect them to die!' There is a cat owned – and stroked – by the villain in the manner of Donald Pleasance's Ernst Blofeld; there is a plot to steal nuclear arms and use them for global blackmail. There is a vast hideout inside a volcano; an

assassin modelled on Robert Shaw's Red Grant in the movie *From Russia With Love*; and a female thug who is a combination of those two Bond harridans – Rosa Klebb (*From Russia With Love*) and Irma Bunt (*On Her Majesty's Secret Service*). Some of the settings, such as Las Vegas, bear direct similarity to those in the 007 movies. Even Myers' obscene doormat of artificial chest hair is allegedly modelled on Sean Connery's.

Will there be further adventures for the toothsome and bespectacled Powers? Perhaps not. As one reviewer commented after the last movie, '[There's] only so much Bond-baiting to be done…'

Las Vegas

Johnny English
A thoroughly English satire

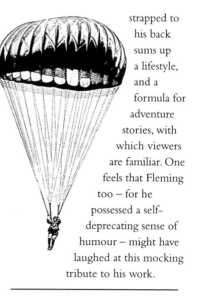

The most up-to-date satire was that of the *Johnny English* movies, starring Rowan Atkinson. Set in the present day, they involve a character that Atkinson has made his own – that of the small man who dreams of success.

A minor member of the British Secret Service MI7, he gets his big break in the first movie *Johnny English* (2003), when all the other agents are assassinated at a funeral, leaving him as the only hope of saving Britain. In this, and its sequel *Johnny English Reborn* (2011), Atkinson makes good use of the opportunities that the clichés provide, with a host of gadgets that go wrong and plenty of visual humour based upon the inept handling of pistols, cigarettes and other props.

Once again, the cultural references are so well known that members of the audience can pick them up even if they were not born when the early Bond movies were released. A poster for the movie showing the agent in a dinner jacket but with a parachute strapped to his back sums up a lifestyle, and a formula for adventure stories, with which viewers are familiar. One feels that Fleming too – for he possessed a self-deprecating sense of humour – might have laughed at this mocking tribute to his work.

LIQUORICE CABLE

Richard Keil, who played the formidable Jaws in **The Spy Who Loved Me** *and* **Moonraker**, *found his trademark steel teeth so agonising to wear that he could only do so for a matter of minutes at a time. In the latter production he was required to bite through a steel cable, but found this relatively painless – it was actually made of liquorice!*

Spoof version
Why 1967's Casino
Royale *was slapstick*

One of the best Bond novels, *Casino Royale,* was initially brought to the screen as a slapstick production because EON Productions did not possess movie rights for the book. The novel *Casino Royale* had, of course, some very photogenic scenes, and would have made a most exciting movie – although the incident in which Bond is tortured would not have been acceptable to the censors and audiences in any country in the 1960s. Nevertheless, there was public expectation that, as the first of the novels, it would appear on the screen and the man who *did* acquire the rights, Charles K. Feldman, was keen to produce it.

EON had already stamped the Bond movies with its own characteristics and was really the only company that could carry on the genre without the risk of a loss of style and continuity. Feldman therefore approached Salzman and Broccoli to see if the movie could be made as a joint venture. Sadly, the two parties could not agree. Rather than sell the rights to EON – they would surely have paid well for them – and let them add *Royale* to their stable, Feldman decided to produce the movie himself. He knew he could not compete with EON on its own terms, so he decided to play the movie for laughs and make a spoof of the 007 cult. After all, others were doing the same. He could carry out the task more effectively because he had the legal right to use original names and concepts.

The movie was released in 1967 and was a venture that serious fans would like to forget. It was bad by any standards, and for several reasons. Its greatest problem was in the making – it had five different directors, each responsible for a single segment. These had been written by a host of different people whose ideas naturally did not match, and

somehow the sections had to be grafted together and given coherence. Although some of the writers – Billy Wilder and Woody Allen, for instance – were comic writers of proven success and undoubted talent, the result was an atrocious mish-mash that was very difficult for audiences or critics to understand. The only strength of the movie was that it used a large number of high-calibre actors whose performances sprinkled it with a little lustre: David Niven, Ursula Andress, Woody Allen and William Holden. Nevertheless it was a success at the box office.

Mass mayhem
The madcap plot of 1967's Casino Royale *movie*

In Ian Fleming's novel *Casino Royale*, a French trade union boss (and Soviet agent) – Le Chiffre – has embezzled his organisation's funds, which were provided by Russia. To recover his loss before the Kremlin finds out, he resorts to desperate gambling. Bond is sent to a casino Le Chiffre frequents in order to defeat him at the tables, thus bankrupting

his opponent and laying him open to revenge and removal by Russia's secret service. The plot of Wolf Mankowitz, John Law and Michael Sayers's 1967 movie version of *Casino Royale* was implausible even by the standards of a send-up, although the basic notion was more or less sound. Bond (now Sir James, and played by David Niven), long retired from the Secret Service and living in a country house, is asked to return to duty. This has been the starting point for viable movie plots in the past; the reason here is in order to investigate the disappearance of a number of spies. He is asked not only by M but by the KGB and the French Secret Service. He refuses, and in a sulk his erstwhile colleagues then subject his home to a mortar attack. Bond survives but M is killed and Bond is subsequently appointed as M's replacement. He decides that henceforth all MI6 agents will be re-named 'James Bond' and will all carry the number 007, so that targeting the original will be far more difficult.

The action centres on the casino that, it transpires, conceals beneath it the underground headquarters of the movie's villain, Doctor Noah. This man, who predictably wishes to destroy the world, proves in the end to be none other than 007's nephew Jimmy Bond, a person of short stature whose dream is to eliminate all men taller than 4ft 6in (1.4m), thus removing any competition and becoming attractive to women. Also featured are 007's previously unknown daughter Mata Bond and a young woman with the wonderful name – worthy of Fleming himself – of Miss Goodthighs. While some names are fanciful, others are used with all the confidence of a copyright holder: for example, there is a villain called Le Chiffre, played by Orson Welles.

The movie, which was appropriately described by critics as 'madcap', includes several scenes of mass mayhem and a free-for-all fight in the casino at the end. Unlike the serious Bond movies, in which the world is saved, this one ends in disaster when Jimmy Bond's nuclear pill explodes, sending him to hell while his illustrious uncle, and various others, go to heaven. The movie is an agreeable romp for those who like dated humour or a 1960s atmosphere, or who admire the comedic acting of the stars in it, and don't mind the liberties taken with a venerable thriller.

Artistic licence
The town that never was

Royale-les-Eaux, the northern French seaside resort that features in the novels *Casino Royale* and *On Her Majesty's Secret Service*, does not exist. It is based on a combination of similar 'watering places' such as Deauville, Trouville and Le Touquet that Fleming and his circle would have known during the 1930s. By 1953, when *Casino Royale* was published, the war and economic hardship had cost such towns much of their glamour and many of their regular visitors.

The attempt by Bulgarian assassins in the novel to kill Bond with a bomb on behalf of the Russians would have been the most exciting event in the town's recent history. The incident itself was not completely invented – a similar thing had happened, but in wartime Istanbul and not in peacetime France. The intended victim was the German Ambassador, Franz von Papen and, as in Fleming's book, the would-be killers were Bulgarians. In both instances they blew themselves up instead of their target. Fleming knew a good deal about the attempt on Papen, and decided it would make a useful scene in his novel.

Inventing an entire location for a story was a technique that Fleming did not repeat after this first novel. A talented travel writer with a gift for capturing the essence of a place, he realised that using – and giving detailed descriptions of – real and exotic locations would greatly enhance the appeal of his stories.

DISLOYAL TO ROYALE

When **Casino Royale** *appeared in paperback in the US, the novel was given the title* **You Asked For It.** *This was because the publishers at the time had feared that Americans would not know how to pronounce 'Royale'.*

Stranger than fiction
A topical reference lost on audiences today

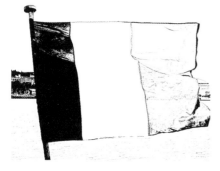

One of the most notorious art thefts of the decade was solved by James Bond in the movie *Dr No.* Unfortunately, Bond got the wrong man …

In the spring of 1961, British newspapers lamented the fact that a painting of great national importance was about to go overseas. The portrait of the Duke of Wellington by the great Spanish artist Francesco de Goya (1746–1828) had been painted from life after Wellington's armies had driven the French invaders out of Spain. It was a sincere tribute from a Spanish artist grateful for the liberation of his country, and was a flattering likeness.

Charles Wrightsman, a US collector, had bought the portrait and paid the sum of £140,000 for the canvas. However there was a public outcry at the prospect that it would be lost to the nation. The government duly stepped in, raised precisely the same sum and bought the painting for the British people. It was subsequently hung in London's National Gallery.

Not all British citizens were happy with this outcome. Kempton Bunton

The National Gallery, London

(1900–76) was a bus driver on a very low income. What he resented most about his poverty was having to pay for a television licence, and he was incensed that the government should be throwing away such a sum on a single painting. Three months after Goya's portrait went on display, it suddenly vanished; it would be missing for four years.

While the authorities, and the public, speculated that the theft was the work of a sophisticated gang of international art thieves, the truth was more prosaic: Bunton had taken it. His actions had been beautifully simple. He had visited the gallery and, in conversation with the guards, had discovered that the infrared sensors that protected the picture were actually de-activated early in the mornings so that cleaning staff could work without setting off the alarm.

The back of the Gallery looks onto a small thoroughfare – Orange Street – that is extremely quiet during much of the day. On the morning of 26 August 1961 Bunton, apparently with little difficulty, climbed in through a window before the premises were open and simply lifted the picture, frame and all, off the wall. He climbed back into the street and was gone.

Bunton lived in north-east England and for the next few years the portrait was kept in the back of his wardrobe. He had no interest in owning, or even keeping it. He had in fact intended to demand a ransom, and he had lost little time in sending his terms in a letter to Reuter's news agency. He wanted, he said anonymously, a donation to charity of £140,000 that would be used to buy television licences for the poor; he also wanted an amnesty for himself. There was no official response. His terms were ignored and years passed without official news of the painting.

Bunton became tired of the fuss his action had caused and, more importantly, he grew increasingly concerned about having such a valuable object in his possession, especially since he had failed to secure the terms he wanted. By 1965 he had had enough. He wrote to the *Daily Mirror* newspaper, enclosing a paper ticket, and told them the picture would be found at the left luggage office in Birmingham's New Street Station. Indeed it was,

although it lacked its frame and could only be positively identified once art experts had examined marks on the back of the canvas.

Six weeks later, Bunton turned himself in at a police station. The officers, seeing in front of them an elderly and overweight man (he was 61 and weighed 17 stone) were initially sceptical, but in due course the man was arrested and put on trial. His defence argued successfully that he had not intended to keep the painting, and in fact he could be charged solely with stealing the frame – worth only a few pounds. He was subsequently sentenced to three months in prison. In 1968 the law was changed to enable anyone carrying out a similar action to be more vigorously prosecuted.

What has this to do with 007? Simply that in the movie *Dr No*, when Bond and Honeychile Rider are first captured and then invited to dine with Dr No, they step out of the elevator into his open-plan undersea living quarters and there, in front of them, is Goya's painting. No wonder Bond does a double take! The audiences must have howled with laughter. Dr No – at least the figure described by Fleming in the novel – was 6.5ft (2m) tall and completely hairless, even to the extent of lacking eyelashes. He dressed in a grey silk Chinese robe and had two steel pincers instead of hands. It is wonderful to imagine that police, summoned to the National Gallery in the wake of the theft, might have asked: 'Did you see anyone suspicious-looking...'

The version of the portrait used in the movie was in fact painted in the space of a single weekend by production designer Ken Adam, who based it on a slide of the original obtained from the gallery.

NO THANKS

*When the movie version of **Dr No** was made in 1962, the character of Dr No was modified in appearance to the extent that he looked more-or-less normal apart from his black-gloved hands. Fleming suggested that the Doctor should be played by his close friend and near neighbour in Jamaica, Noel Coward. Coward, however, declined. Interestingly, Christopher Lee also turned it down; he would have been very effective in the role and later did appear as a Bond villain, Francesco Scaramanga in **The Man With the Golden Gun**. Joseph Wiseman was subsequently cast as the evil doctor, and gave a splendidly villainous performance in the role.*

Cross-channel raspberry
Bond plays to anti-Gallic sentiment

At the time that the movie *Thunderball* was made in 1965, Britain was still smarting from the refusal of France's President, Charles de Gaulle, to allow the UK to join the Common Market. Anti-Gallic

Charles de Gaulle

feeling ran high, and British cinema audiences would have been absolutely delighted with the movie's pre-credits sequence, chiefly remembered for Bond's escape from the Chateau d'Anet outside Paris. He uses a Bell jet pack, a device that was developed by the US Army but which never came into general use, and this rocket-propelled device enabled him to escape his immediate surroundings but not to get clean away, since it could remain airborne for no more than three or four minutes.

The scene began with a funeral. The initials displayed among the flowers – JB – proved not to be Bond's, as audiences would initially have assumed, but those of Jacques Boitier, a French assassin whose seemingly attractive widow was conspicuously grieving. Bond, suspicious, discovered that she was in fact Boitier in disguise. They fought in hand-to-hand combat and Bond killed his opponent. As the Frenchman, ridiculous and undignified in women's clothing, lay dead in the fireplace, Bond tossed a bouquet of flowers on to his body and departed. One can imagine the cheer that would have gone up from British cinema audiences at the sight of this Gallic ridicule.

Armed to the teeth
007's arsenal of firearms

A s with everything else in a world where reality is suspended, Bond's shooting is impossibly accurate. He can fire without aiming and sometimes without even looking. He can handle unfamiliar weapons without difficulty, has limitless ammunition and can shoot at – or from – a vehicle travelling at high speed with unerring precision.

James Bond is clearly an expert on weaponry, but the same could not be said for his creator. Ian Fleming was several times photographed posing with revolvers, but he knew very little about them and in fact disliked firearms. He did not even enjoy rough-shooting, an almost obligatory pastime among members of his class.

When Fleming began writing his novels he equipped 007 with a small pistol, a Beretta 418. He had decided that this would be a suitable weapon, similar in size to the sidearm, a .25 ACP Beretta, with which he had himself been issued while working for naval intelligence. Fleming had Bond house his weapon in a chamois leather shoulder holster.

In 1956, three years after he had begun to write, Fleming found he had access to expert advice. Opening a fan letter one day, he read that a man living in Scotland, named Geoffrey Boothroyd admired his books but not the weapon employed by his agent. Boothroyd was a gun collector and possessed considerable expertise.

Deriding the Beretta as 'a lady's gun', Boothroyd suggested that Bond instead use a Smith & Wesson Centennial Airweight Revolver and keep it in a Berns-Martin holster which, he said, would make it far easier to draw. He also suggested Bond carry a second, heavier firearm in his car – a .357 Smith & Wesson Magnum. Given that 007 was often up against entire private armies, a single small handgun simply did not have the 'stopping power' the agent would require.

Fleming was grateful for this advice, and took up regular correspondence with Mr Boothroyd. His only quibble with Boothroyd's advice was that he felt Bond should carry an automatic rather than a revolver, which seemed too cumbersome to be carried beneath well-tailored suits or dinner jackets. Boothroyd subsequently recommended the Walther PPK, and this has been the pistol most commonly associated with the 007 character ever since.

Boothroyd was also able to advise on the equipment suitable for Bond's opponents. He felt SMERSH should have different weapons from the

Walther PPK

British agents, and suggested two other types of German-manufactured gun for the organisation: the Luger and the Mauser. Although the Walther was a pistol that had been widely used throughout the Third Reich, the names of the Luger and Mauser were far better known as potent symbols of evil, their names alone carrying a suggestion of menace.

007 IS TIMELESS

Although the Bond cult was a product of the Cold War era, it has maintained its grip on the public imagination even in a post-communist world. Box-office returns for the movies are actually higher than they were during the years of East-West confrontation, showing that the character has proved strong enough to survive the loss of the context for which he was created.

The PPK appears in by far the majority of Bond books and movies. Of the Bond authors, only John Gardner has deviated from established practice by having 007 carry other weapons, including a Browning 9mm, an FN M1903 and a Heckler & Koch VP70, made by another German manufacturer highly regarded by police marksmen throughout the world.

The Walther PPK weighs 21oz (590kg), has a barrel-length of 3.3in (155mm), a width of 1in (25mm), and a height of 3.9in (100mm). It can, in other words, fit comfortably into the palm of the hand – discretion indeed. It fires a 7.65mm cartridge from a magazine with eight bullets and its ammunition can be widely bought, thus ensuring a ready supply regardless of where 007 is operating. The version carried by Bond is precisely the same model that was carried by Adolf Hitler, and with which he later shot himself.

But what of Geoffrey Boothroyd? He and Fleming met, and were photographed together. He proved to be a very dignified-looking man with an impressive moustache, much like everyone's idea of a retired major. Fleming, in fact, was to transform him into precisely that. His thanks for Boothroyd's help was to make him a character in the stories, introducing him in the novel *Dr No* as 'Major Boothroyd', the Secret Service armourer who gives useful advice to Bond on the weapons he should carry. He is described by M as the greatest small-arms expert in the world; fulsome thanks indeed for services rendered.

WELL EQUIPPED

Bond is loaded with devices to save his life and foil his enemies, but these were not initially part of the stories. In both the early books and movies, Bond was not originally dependent on gadgetry. In the movie Dr No, *Sean Connery used nothing more than a pistol, some basic judo holds and a certain amount of creative driving to defeat his opponents. The first time one of Q's inventions made an appearance was in the second movie,* **From Russia With Love,** *in the form of an attaché case containing a concealed knife, 50 gold sovereigns and a tear-gas charge. In the novel, it is the knife that enables Bond to kill his would-be assassin, Red Grant; however in the movie it is the gas charge that stuns Grant and enables Bond to strangle him with yet another gadget – the wire attached to the killer's own watch.*

Bond on wheels
From Bentley to Saab

No single component of Bond's brand of magic is more important than his automobile. If a fast and powerful car is a symbol of virility in a man, in Bond's case this is exaggeratedly obvious. Whatever he drives – and the model, understandably, is periodically updated to ensure that it is state-of-the-art – the vehicle contributes significantly to his screen appeal for both male and female viewers.

The cars have traditionally been petrol-guzzling monsters, able to out-speed anything else on the road, capable of performing nail-biting manoeuvres – flying across gaps, taking corners on two wheels, turning turtle – and of taking ferocious punishment. They must also be expensive enough to be unattainable to most of the audience. They are the very essence of the out-of-reach glamour of the Bond lifestyle.

Although the first car to feature in the novels – the Bentley 4.5 litre – was a treasured possession and was described as Bond's hobby (it must have taken great physical strength to handle), he has never since then been personally attached to the car he drives. Bond's vehicles are customised for his missions by Q's workshop, issued like any other company car and very often written off in the line of duty. No individual automobile, not even the Aston Martin DBS with which he is most associated, is his own personal vehicle.

It is not just the machines that are impressive, but what he gets away with doing while driving them. No one watching his movies, even if they have such a car, is allowed to drive it at speed through urban areas regardless of the consequences. Like the autogyro *Little Nellie*, the jet pack with which he takes off in *Thunderball*, and even the ludicrous 'Bondola' in *Moonraker*, Bond is allowed to play with expensive toys in a way that appeals to the small boy in every man. This, too, is powerful magic.

Bond's road handling is legendary, doubtless honed by numerous defensive driving courses undertaken on the skidpans of the Secret Service and practiced in the field. Yet no matter what destruction he wreaks in his cars, Her Majesty's Government clears up the mess, pays for the damage and deals with all the

Aston Martin DBS

tiresome complaints. The majority of motorists spend their lives boringly, fastidiously obeying traffic laws. The sheer exhilaration of being able to ignore these with cavalier indifference and a clear conscience (Bond is, after all, in the process of saving the world!) must be a heady feeling indeed.

EVEN BOND GETS SPEEDING TICKETS

An unusually realistic note is struck in the movie **A View to a Kill** *following a car chase through Paris in which Bond drives with his customary abandon and causes the usual amount of mayhem. The Secret Service subsequently receives a bill for damages from the local police for 6 million French Francs!*

Cars are of huge importance in the Bond stories; *You Only Live Twice* is the only one in which he does not drive. They are chosen for their sleek outlines, power and manoeuvrability, regardless of the country in which they are made. From using a Bentley in the early novels, Bond has progressed – with an uncharacteristic lack of chauvinism – to BMWs.

The Aston Martin DBS, introduced to cinemagoers in *Goldfinger*, has proved to be the most important Bond car. Its range of gadgets, reproduced in miniature for the Corgi model, captured the imagination of a generation of small boys. A decade later the Lotus Esprit in *The Spy Who Loved Me*, with its ability to travel underwater, similarly won admirers. More recently the BMS Z3 Roadster was a convertible that appeared in *GoldenEye* months before it was on sale to the public. Although talked about a great deal in the movie's publicity, the car did not play a major role in the plot and, although apparently loaded with gadgets in the customary manner, these were not seen in use.

NEWSPRINT WRECKS BENTLEY

*In the novel **Moonraker** Bond's famous Bentley is wrecked when it is struck by a giant roll of newsprint that falls off the back of a lorry while he is driving behind it through the Kent countryside. This had come, readers are told, from the paper mill at Aylesford outside Maidstone – another of the local landmarks Fleming would have known from his journeys to and from the Kent coast. The mill is still in operation today.*

Little Nellie
Bond's versatile miniature aircraft

*L*ittle Nellie was the autogyro flown by 007 in *You Only Live Twice*. Formidably armed with guns and missiles, she sees off attack despite being heavily outnumbered. The craft – which in reality was completely unarmed – was actually constructed and flown in 1966 as a hobby by retired RAF Officer, Wing Commander Ken Wallis.

Harry Salzman, one of the partners who produced the Bond movies, saw it pictured in a magazine and decided it would add interest to his current project. Almost simultaneously the production designer, Ken Adam (himself a former RAF pilot) heard it described on the radio. Both men recognised an opportunity to incorporate a highly original, up-to-the-minute and visually exciting piece of technology into the next Bond movie.

Technicians transformed the craft, adding its distinctive yellow livery as well as the array of weapons. Sean Connery did not fly the autogiro, except in front of a studio backdrop, but the scene was one of the best in the movie and *Little Nellie* was much admired.

MONASTERY PUTS UP A FIGHT

*When the movie **For Your Eyes Only** was being filmed in Kalambaka, Greece, monks at a nearby monastery objected to the noise and disruption caused by the set. They retaliated by hanging up signs that spoiled the camera angles and interfered with shooting.*

Mountaintop retreat
Blofeld's palace draws hungry skiers

In the movie *On Her Majesty's Secret Service* Ernst Blofeld's 'hideaway' (it's hardly inconspicuous!) in the Swiss Alps is in fact a restaurant, which was not yet complete at the time that shooting took place. Its use in the movie was, needless to say, welcome publicity, and it has taken the name – Piz Gloria – that it was given in the story.

'Piz' is the word for 'peak' in the Romansch language that is spoken in some parts of Switzerland – although not in the German-speaking Canton of Bern, where the restaurant is located. The movie was supposedly set in the area near St Moritz, although the mountaintops around Piz Gloria are unmistakable to anyone who knows

Piz Gloria, Swiss Alps

Switzerland. The building itself – the work of a local architect named Konrad Wolf – was used in the story by Ernst Blofeld as a clinic for those suffering from allergies. It was the first revolving restaurant in the country (there are now two others) and has claims to be the oldest in the world, although in fact Seattle in the US has one that dates from the World's Fair of 1962.

Piz Gloria sits on top of one of Switzerland's great mountains – the Schilthorn – at a height of 9,744ft (2,970m) above sea level, near the village of Murren in the Bernese Oberland. It is reached by a cableway that is the largest in the Alps and at the top of this visitors find a viewing platform that is large enough to allow a helicopter to land. The outlook includes numerous lakes and more than 200 other peaks including the Eiger, the Monch, the Jungfrau and – in the far distance – Mont Blanc. If the day is sufficiently clear it is possible to see as far as the Black Forest in Germany.

The building itself is on two storeys, the higher of which is a restaurant that turns on a core of 12ft (3.7m) diameter. It takes 55 minutes – the length of a leisurely luncheon – to complete a revolution and, following a refurbishment since the movie was made, can seat 400 people. Owing to the difficulties of building at such a height, the restaurant was assembled from prefabricated parts that were lifted to the peak. The roof was originally coated with aluminium, although this was subsequently replaced.

The moviemakers took over the site before work was finished, and financially contributed towards the cost of completing the building in return for its use. Few restaurants anywhere can have had a better start in life than to be the principal setting for a major movie, or been offered a more attractive and sophisticated theme, and from the beginning Piz Gloria has drawn serious Bond

pilgrims as well as the idly curious. There is no likelihood that any visitor will go away having failed to realise its connection with 007.

Apart from the name, the bill of fare offers some crashingly obvious clues, for some refreshments are made to the agent's specifications. The staff in the James Bond Bar will swiftly produce a martini unstirred enough to gratify 007 himself. If you pop into the restaurant between 8 and 11 o'clock in the morning you can order a 'James Bond Breakfast' that includes everything except the Scottish housekeeper. And for lunch there is something called 'Spaghetti James Bond' – although this suggests creativity on the part of the management since there is no mention, in either novels or movies, of 007 being fond of the dish.

Otherwise there is a display of memorabilia, and there are opportunities to see extracts from the movie – including the exciting shoot-out when Draco's men capture the building. Even the restaurant's phone number – 3382 60 007 – is evocative of the Bond brand.

PINK PANTHER

Bert Kwouk, a Chinese-British actor best known for his performance as Kato in the Pink Panther movies, appeared as a henchman of villainous Blofeld in the movie You Only Live Twice.

Home from home
Pinewood Studios, the 007 stage

Pinewood Studios, situated outside London, is the largest sound stage in Europe. It has witnessed some of 007's most spectacular scenes, as well as being used by other production companies for the making of their own epics.

Pinewood was originally a wealthy man's country estate called Heatherden. Situated just over 20 miles (32km) west of London in the Buckinghamshire countryside at Iver Heath, it was a short drive from the capital. In 1934 it was transformed by Charles Boot, a member of the British pharmaceutical family, into an exclusive country club, but was almost at once to take on another function

– and one that would ultimately make it famous throughout the world.

In 1936 Boot's partner in the venture, J. Arthur Rank, conceived the idea of setting up a movie studio on the estate. The house itself, Heatherden Hall, was left intact and converted into offices for producers and other executives, while the extensive grounds were partially built upon. The movie-making facilities, here as in Hollywood, consisted of both indoor sound stages and a 'back lot' for outdoor work. The studio was named Pinewood for two reasons: the first part was instantly apparent to visitors in the wealth of fir trees that grew in this sandy soil; the second was a reference to the world's movie capital, Hollywood.

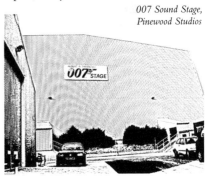

007 Sound Stage, Pinewood Studios

The studio quickly became both busy and famous, and has remained so ever since, gradually expanding as the needs of the industry became more complex, as technical equipment became more sophisticated and as productions became bigger and more spectacular. The house and grounds have, over the years, been glimpsed in movies as background (Heatherden Hall was actually used as a setting in the comedy *Carry On Up the Khyber*) but it is the make-believe world, built on Pinewood's sets, that possesses the real magic.

The Bond movies began their long association with Pinewood with the filming of *Dr No* in February and March 1962. Almost all of them have used the site, and as producers' demands have increased so too have the facilities they have had built. The Bond legacy is now obvious to anyone who enters Pinewood, for the largest single structure in the complex, the Albert R. Broccoli 007 Stage (it is the size and shape of an aircraft hangar) displays, high up on its wall, the famous 007 pistol logo.

Bond movies, and innumerable other productions, will continue to be made at Pinewood Studios for many years to come. The physical plant will remain although it may not need to expand further, for computer technology has made it increasingly possible to create the effects of space, complex backgrounds and hordes of people without the need for these things to be physically present. Nevertheless Pinewood, which has merged with Shepperton Studios to create an immense co-ordinated movie-making plant, can today offer 35 studios, together with thousands of specialist staff that include some of the world's most expert movie technicians. James Bond will not be looking for a new home anytime soon.

Apocalyptic
Story of a sound stage

Pinewood's largest sound stage is actually the third to occupy its site. The first was created for the making of *The Spy Who Loved Me* (1977). There was no stage of suitable size for filming the pivotal plot scene, set inside the gigantic belly of the tanker *Liparus*, so Cubby Brocccoli decided that the obvious solution was to build his own. The building's opening was attended by the former British Prime Minister Harold Wilson; having been premier during the years in which *Goldfinger, Thunderball* and *On Her Majesty's Secret Service* were made Wilson was, in theory, the man to whom M would have reported and who would have authorised those missions.

At the time, the statistics of this sound stage – the largest ever constructed – commanded considerable respect. It made available some 45,424ft/sq (4,220m/sq) of filming space and contained a tank measuring 297ft (91m) in length, which was 73ft (22.5m) wide and more than 8ft (2.7m) deep. It was built specifically to accommodate the tanker *Liparus* with which the villainous Karl Stromberg (played by Curt Jurgens) captured nuclear submarines from the world's oceans. The interior of *Liparus* had to be capable of holding three such vessels – and nuclear submarines are themselves huge. The result was a visually spectacular movie – and audience expectations had now been pushed even higher.

Naturally the stage was not needed all the time for Bond movies, and was rented by other production companies. In 1984 the building, however, was destroyed. It burnt down following the explosion of gas canisters, which caused an apocalyptic blaze worthy of a Bond movie. Undaunted EON rebuilt it, indeed work began when the embers were scarcely cold. Within four months the stage was back in operation and shooting of the next Bond movie, *A View to a Kill*, was not the slightest bit delayed.

Movie sets are, unfortunately, highly flammable places, and this is especially true where special effects are concerned. The 007 stage went up in flames a second time in 2006, burning for an hour and a half, just after the filming of the modern *Casino Royale* movie and while the final set, the Venetian palace, was being taken down. In neither of these instances were there, thankfully, any casualties. This time damage had not been as total, but the roof had partly collapsed. It was decided to pull down what remained and undertake a comprehensive reconstruction which, with the same briskness that had been seen previously, began within four days of the fire. The destruction of the old building provided an opportunity to further improve the facilities, and indeed to make the space even bigger.

The new version, formally titled Albert R. Broccoli's 007 Stage, sits on the same footprint as the old one, yet it offers 59,000ft/sq of space (5,500m/sq) – 15,000 more square feet than its predecessor. The tank is bigger, and has a ramp that enables easier access. The stage is now 374ft (114m) long, 158ft (48m) wide and almost 50ft (15m) high.

TOKYO TIGER

The character of Tiger Tanaka, the Japanese man who introduces Bond to the ways of his country in the novel **You Only Live Twice***, was based on a journalist called Tarao Saito (known as Tiger) who performed the same service for Ian Fleming when the author visited Tokyo to gather material for the book.*

Post script
Fleming's other literary exploits

Fleming produced several books besides his 14 Bond novels. In 1957 he wrote *The Diamond Smugglers*, and in 1963 a series of travel vignettes, some based on his recollections and others on visits undertaken specially for the Bond series, published under the title *Thrilling Cities*. The subject matter, writing style and approach of both were all strongly suggestive of James

Bond's world, reflecting the author's love of gambling and penchant for raffish, underworld settings.

Thrilling Cities was issued in paperback as two volumes. One covered Europe and described Fleming's sweeping travels through Hamburg, Berlin, Monte Carlo, Vienna, Geneva, Naples and Capri. The other covered North America and Asia; this time the author visited Hong Kong, Macau, Tokyo, Honolulu, Los Angeles, Las Vegas, Chicago and New York. Another travel book, *Jamaica*, was cobbled together after Fleming's death from a collection of pieces he had written about the island, almost entirely travel articles for various newspapers and magazines.

Although these travel writings are largely unread a better-known work, representing a single but significant change from Fleming's usual formula, was a children's book called *Chitty-Chitty-Bang-Bang*. Many gems of juvenile literature have been written for an author's own children, and Fleming wrote this for his son Caspar, basing the content on bedtime stories he had told him. It was subsequently made into a movie produced by Cubby Broccoli, who had acquired the rights along with those to the Bond movies.

It has been pointed out that this is simply Bond for children, the story involving a gadget-filled car, a secret mission abroad, and even a mad foreign villain – the preposterous Baron Bomburst – played by none other than the old 007 stalwart, Gert Fröbe who played the character Goldfinger. In any event, it proved extremely popular and it comes as a great surprise to many that the creator of Bond also penned this children's classic.

COMIC HERO

James Bond has appeared as a comic strip in the British press: drawn by John McLusky, it was published in the **Sunday Express** *and the* **Daily Star.** *A full-length colour strip of Bond was also produced in the US by DC Comics, the company that had given comic heroes Superman and Batman to the world.*

Must haves
The world of Bond collectables

The Bond movies have been accompanied by a wealth of toys, souvenirs and promotional gimmicks that represent serious money to both those who manufacture them and those who invest in them. Although Disney had been for some years producing items connected with its own movies and retailing them through its Disneyland outlets, the Bond franchise was the first to produce collectables and memorabilia aimed at both adults and children (who could only see the movies if accompanied by an adult). And while the *Star Wars* movies would probably break records for sheer tonnage of goods produced, the Bond collectables have proved to be a lucrative business for the holders of the Bond copyright.

The process of marketing this movie-related merchandise started gradually. For the movie *Dr No*, only the soundtrack was released as a record. The same happened for the movie *From Russia With Love*, although a toy attaché case – Bond's original gadget – was produced retroactively. After the release of *Goldfinger* in 1964, there were two series of bubble-gum cards, all showing black-and-white stills from the movies. One was devoted solely to *Goldfinger*, the other to the two films that had preceded it. A set of *Goldfinger* cards currently costs £185.

It was the next movie, *Thunderball*, that actually introduced a new era of Bond marketing: 1965, the year of the movie's release, saw the introduction of a *James Bond Annual*, a cap pistol in a gold shoulder holster, an action figure of Bond, and one of the character Oddjob that could fling its bowler hat. Best of

all – and the most enduring – was the Corgi model Aston Martin DBS with its bullet-proof shield at the rear, machine guns mounted on the fender and – even more exciting – the ejector seat that could, at the flick of a lever, send a small plastic figure pinging heavenward. This has proved the most popular toy car of all time. And for any boy who had the wisdom, or self-discipline, to look after this toy, there were financial rewards. A Corgi Aston Martin DBS, dating from the 1960s and in near-mint condition, is currently on sale on the Internet at £245, 'less than half the normal price' according to the respected business vendor. This includes a replica box and cardboard display stand that are apparently so similar to the originals that 'only an expert could tell the difference'.

BUBBLE-GUM CARDS BANNED

The series of 60 bubble-gum cards showing stills from the first three Bond films was avidly collected by young fans, but had to be withdrawn following complaints from their parents that too many of the images depicted women in bikinis. This was true; their general state of semi-nudity, as well as their come-hither pouts, bore some resemblance to adult men's magazines of the time.

The tide of promotional toys continued to flow. The release of *You Only Live Twice* fostered a construction-kit of *Little Nellie*, the autogyro that featured in the movie, and Bond's other transport, a Toyota 2000GT, was produced in miniature by Corgi. Vehicles continued to be the most common children's collectable (bobsleds accompanied the release of *On Her Majesty's Secret Service*) while adults could buy the soundtrack album and a reissue of the novel. Enthusiasts assembled posters, stills and other publicity items. It made no difference who played Bond, the props the agent used had taken on a life of their own.

By the time *The Man With the Golden Gun* was released in 1974, promotional merchandise included toiletries by Fabergé, something that would appeal to the refined rather than the 'anorak'. *The Spy Who Loved Me* saw a model of Bond's Lotus Esprit hit the shops, another Corgi product, and over 1.5 million of them were sold in the space of four years; in the US there was even a toy version that worked underwater. The trend continued with *Moonraker*: the scaled-down space shuttle from this movie sold massively, as did the space gun. Perhaps the most unusual toy was a replica of the spin saw that appeared in *Octopussy*.

And so it has gone on. As well as toys there have continued to be more sophisticated collectables – key rings, cuff links, personal organisers, clothes, radios, watches, and computer games. There is also a practice of issuing either novels or DVDs about the making of each movie, since audiences love to learn about developments behind the scenes.

While these things give pleasure to the ordinary collector, there are others for whom they are not enough, and what matters are the actual props used in the movies themselves. In 1998 a number of these were sold at auction at Christies, London, and the prices commanded by some of them were staggering. Roger Moore's watch from *Live and Let Die*, a Rolex Oyster Perpetual, the one with which he unzipped a woman's dress in one of the scenes, sold for £22,000. Meanwhile, the Lotus Esprit he drove in *The Spy Who Loved Me* made £28,000. While the buyer of this was at least getting a whole car, someone else paid £31,000 just for Bond's personal 007 number plate. Oddjob's bowler hat, one of the most important pieces of headgear in cinema history, pushed bidding up to £68,000. Finally, in November 2011 at Christie's in Geneva, Roger

Rolex Oyster Perpetual Watch

Moore's Rolex Oyster Perpetual from *Live And Let Die* sold for over £151,000, a staggering increase in value from the 1998 auction. Such is the magic of Bond.

BOND AND BIKINIS

The appearance of Ursula Andress wearing a bikini in the movie **Dr No** *led to a worldwide increase in the sale of this swimwear garment.*

Golden years
The lifestyle of a retired Bond

In November 1985 the British *Daily Mail* newspaper published an article by Sam Usher imagining what Bond's experiences would be like as a pensioner. As Bond wakes up on his 65th birthday, Usher describes the scene as the retired agent grumbles inwardly – he lives alone and talks to himself a great deal – about the changes in his life. He now suffers from rheumatism, and wears dentures and a hearing aid.

He has to bang on the floor to complain about loud rastafarian music played by his downstairs neighbour. He still lives in Chelsea, but is only able to keep his flat in the 'plane-tree'd square' by renting out some of the rooms, subsisting on a Civil Service pension that has been eroded by rising costs. He has, unsurprisingly, had to get rid of his famous Bentley and has been offered a Sinclair C5 in part-exchange. He now travels by bus, although this does not greatly matter because he no longer ventures outside London. A member of M's old club, Blades, he has fallen behind with his subscription, and no doubt receives increasingly frosty letters from the club secretary.

His days of smoking and drinking are a distant memory, and now the very thought of a dry martini brings on an attack of dyspepsia. As for the famous breakfasts of scrambled eggs and strong black coffee, they have long vanished in favour of muesli and dry toast. His 'Scottish treasure', May the housekeeper, would not have approved of such fare, but he now understands the damage this high-cholesterol diet has done

him and reflects ruefully that the housekeeper might well have been an assassin sent by the Kremlin.

Undoubtedly Usher's most intriguing revelation is that Bond has been married, since he is now described as a widower. Readers would doubtless love to know who his wife was, in what circumstances she managed to snare him, and how she died. Was she killed off to repay a grudge by one of her husband's former opponents, or did his pistol simply go off with disastrous results when he was cleaning it at home one evening?

Whatever the miseries of Bond's circumstances he is cheered up, on going out, to find a 65th birthday card on the doormat. It is a reminder that not everyone has forgotten him. Sent by his old opponents at SMERSH and SPECTRE (perhaps these organisations too are having

to cut costs by sending joint cards!) it wishes him a Happy Birthday, although it hopes there will not be too many more of them. It contains an exploding device that also lets off a whiff of poisonous gas.

It is of course unlikely that Bond would have reached this old age. Quite apart from the danger in which he regularly found himself, his eating, drinking and smoking habits, as well as the mental and physical stress under which he lived, would not have made for a long life. It is more feasible perhaps to assume that James Bond, like his creator, would have died of heart failure while in his mid-50s.

Held in trust
Bond's legacy lives on

Fleming assigned the copyright for his books to Glidrose Productions, which was thus entitled to go on making Bond movies even after Fleming's original material had run out. Fleming had foreseen this possibility, and told Cubby Broccoli: 'Just try to have the scripts written the way I have done in my early books.' The company, first known as Glidrose Productions, then Glidrose Publications and finally as Ian Fleming Publications Ltd, was bought by Fleming in 1952 and used to manage his literary estate. Its name derived from its two founders, John Glidden and Norman Rose, but it is today run by the Fleming family. It continues to negotiate publication and translation rights, and commission new work about Ian Fleming's characters. In recent years it has not only appointed authors for new 007 novels but has enabled writers to approach the subject from unusual angles. These include Charlie Higson, who created a series of books about a youthful James Bond, and Samantha Weinberg (writing as 'Kate Westbrook'), who had the original, and successful, notion of producing *The Moneypenny Diaries*.

As a fictional hero, James Bond will continue to flourish. Ian Fleming Publications Ltd continues to commission writers to produce stories about the adult character, the latest being Sebastian Faulks with his novel *Devil May Care*. Because the plots are somewhat formulaic and the audience has a set of well-defined expectations, the books can be written with considerable success even by authors not used to producing thrillers. There is no reason why the Bond adventures, in the form of both novels and movies, should not still be appearing in a hundred years' time.

WHO'S YOUR FAVOURITE?
Public opinion is as fickle as ever when it comes to choosing the best Bond. One poll by the James Bond International Fan Club in 2011 found that Piers Brosnan was the most popular of the six actors who have played the role; he won 31% of the vote. Sean Connery came a respectable second

with 29%, then Daniel Craig
with 25%, Roger Moore with 9%,
Timothy Dalton with 6% and
George Lazenby with a lowly 2%.

Dynamic successors
Bond literary adventures
to continue

Four years after Fleming's death, the trustees of his estate sought to continue the Bond genre by commissioning other authors to write further adventures. The reasons were twofold: firstly, there was a tendency for writers to produce works about the agent without permission. They were free to use the name, and legal action could only be taken if the books pretended to be connected in some way with Fleming. It made sense to curb this trend by appointing an 'official' author who could work with the blessing of the estate. Secondly, there was still undoubtedly mileage to be had from the character and from the style of the plots.

PSEUDONYM
It was originally envisaged that there would be a single pseudonym for the new Bond creators, but a succession of authors. It was suggested that this should be 'George Glidrose' in reference to the company, Glidrose Publications Ltd that looked after the rights, although in the end Robert Markham was the name chosen. In the event there was to be only one writer, and one novel, under this name: **Colonel Sun** *was published in 1969 and was the work of Kingsley Amis.*

Lucky Jim
Kingsley Amis picks
up the Bond baton

Kingsley Amis (1922–1995) was at first glance an unlikely recruit to the world of Ian Fleming and James Bond. The son of a minor clerk, his background contained none of the well-connected privilege that had instilled in Fleming such a sense of flippant entitlement, and he had no affiliation with the world of espionage. As a writer he had seen himself as a poet (he was a close friend of Philip Larkin) more than a novelist, but his satire of life in red-brick academia, *Lucky Jim* (1954) established him overnight as one of the most gifted members of a new generation of comedic writers, and henceforth he concentrated more on fiction than poetry.

Amis' writing dealt largely with a world that Fleming would not have recognised and in which he would not wish to have moved – the author's situations and characters, although funny and well-drawn, were of studied ordinariness, and his outlook was one of unromantic realism. He was viewed as having effectively caught the mood of Britain in the decades that followed World War II, but it was not the same country as that in which Ian Fleming and his friends lived.

Like millions throughout the world, Amis admired the novels of Ian Fleming. He enjoyed their escapism, their sophistication, their well-constructed plots and their nuanced, tongue-in-cheek English snobbery. *The James Bond Dossier*, which he

wrote in 1965, was a genuine tribute to the work of a writer whom many critics considered a literary lightweight. In it Amis presented an intelligent analysis of the Bond character, his world and his tastes.

However Amis was also capable of sending up the whole genre, as he did in a wicked and anonymous little publication entitled *The Book of Bond, or Every Man His Own 007*. This was written for Jonathan Cape, the publishers of Fleming's novels, and was famously given a dust jacket that stated the book was *The Bible Designed to be Read as Literature*, the same title as the hollowed-out volume in which, in *Goldfinger*, Bond conceals his Walther PPK and its Berns-Martin holster. Not the least funny thing about this book is that it is so small – 112 pages thick and less than 0.5in (1.3cm) wide – that no weapon could possibly be hidden inside it.

These publications had established Amis as an authentic fan of, and a serious authority on, the Bond books. That he was regarded as such was proved by the fact that, when preparing to issue the novel *The Man With the Golden Gun* after

Fleming's death, the publishers asked Amis to read the manuscript and comment on why it was so weak. He had started to look increasingly like a natural successor...

Not everyone, however, was in favour of Amis continuing the series. Fleming's wife Ann was horrified. She herself had been no great admirer of the character her husband had invented, and she did not see the point of writing further books about him. Bond was, she said, Ian's creation, and she disliked not only the notion of others dabbling with him but the increasing commercialisation of the 007 brand. When Amis' *Colonel Sun* appeared in 1969, the *Sunday Telegraph* asked her to review it. She did, but was so savagely dismissive of the book that the article was not published.

Ann Fleming not only disliked the choice of author but what she called the 'exploiters' of Bond's image. She regarded Amis, with upper class disdain, as likely to portray a petit bourgeois, red-brick Bond who would lack the sophistication admired by her husband's readers, and to transform the character into a cheap parody. No doubt her views on the

subsequent authors employed to extend the life of Bond would have been equally pungent. Amis, for his part, bore her no grudge; he admitted to being happy to write the book for such generous remuneration.

Golden pen
The prolific John Gardner

John Gardner (1926–2007), a thriller writer of considerable accomplishment with a string of original characters to his name, was to write more Bond novels than Ian Fleming himself.

Gardner began writing novels during the spy-story mania of the 1960s, and his work met with immediate success. His first book, *The Liquidator* (1964) was made into a movie that was released when Bond fever was still infecting cinema audiences. The fun it poked at the spying profession was a welcome relief after years in which the subject had either been treated with excessive realism or had been impossibly over-glamourised.

Gardner had also proved successful in breathing new life into a character already created by someone else, for he wrote three books about Professor Moriarty, the villain in Arthur Conan Doyle's *Sherlock Holmes* stories. This suggested he could take on the mindset of another writer without descending into pastiche or parody; subsequently in 1981 he was asked by Glidrose Productions Ltd to write a James Bond novel.

In all he was to produce 16 of them, if one counts the novelised screenplays of two movies – *Licence to Kill* and *GoldenEye*. His work was well regarded by fans and took the character to a new level – older, more careful of his health, more conscious of the environment, and more weary of the world in which his profession has forced him to live. Gardner kept the plots up to date as Glasnost arrived, the Cold War thawed with increasing momentum and communism collapsed to be succeeded by other threats. He also introduced real personalities – notably President Mikhail Gorbachev – in a way that Fleming had not.

Perhaps he felt he faced more of a struggle than his predecessor had done in holding public attention amid

Mikhail Gorbachev

the distractions of changing fashion in books and cinema. After a break of several years from 1996 Gardner returned to writing and produced, in 2001, a final Bond novel, *Day of Absolution*. His death, at the age of 80, was swift and sudden, if sadly prosaic for a man who had so extensively both experienced and written about action – he collapsed while out shopping in the Hampshire town of Basingstoke. He had died of heart failure – as had Ian Fleming.

An unlikely successor
Raymond Benson, the first US Bond writer

Next to be asked to take to the steering wheel of the Bond legacy was Raymond Benson (1955–), at first glance an unlikely successor. Gardner had, like Fleming, been of the generation that served in World War II, and could be assumed to share at least experiences and attitudes with Bond. He also had a background – at Oxbridge and in the Services – that made him familiar with the speech, thought and behaviour of the British Establishment.

However Benson was an American from Texas, and had been born in

Raymond Benson

1955 during the years that the original novels were being written. He was commissioned on the strength of his commercially successful book, *The James Bond Bedside Companion*, which was published in 1984 and reissued four years later. Highly regarded within the thriller-writing fraternity, this was nominated for an award by the Mystery Writers of America.

Benson was to write six Bond novels and to undertake the novelisation of three movies of the Pierce Brosnan era: *Tomorrow Never Dies, The World is Not Enough* and *Die Another Day.* He also wrote some short stories about 007, a thing that Fleming but none of his successors had done. These were to be collected and published, although not until several years after he had progressed to other areas.

Benson's Bond was credible and effective and, as a gifted writer and composer, he was unhappy about devoting his career to following in the literary footsteps of another, no matter how much this enhanced his reputation. In 2002 he was willing to part from Ian Fleming Publications Ltd.

A new dimension
The innovative Charlie Higson

Charles (Charlie) Higson (1958–), too, was not an obvious choice for a Bond author. Although he had written several novels he had no pedigree regarding espionage or thrillers, and was far better known as a writer of scripts for – and participant in – the 1990s television comedy series *The Fast Show*.

Nevertheless he achieved the most innovative angle yet on the subject of 007 by returning to the agent's youth and setting his adventures in the world of adolescence. Since the surroundings of an English public school (Higson uses Eton as the setting rather than Fettes, where Bond spent much more

Charlie Higson

time) do not offer sufficient scope for villainy on the scale that a usual Bond story requires, there are visits to London as well as travel, during the holidays, throughout the UK and abroad, thus enabling the ubiquitous exotic locations to be introduced.

The books are fast paced and exciting, and they have made serious fans of an entire age group that previously thought of Bond only in terms of collectables. The Ian Fleming Foundation was interested to explore this new departure, commissioning a series of the books rather than starting with just one to test public reaction, and their bold gamble paid off. There were a further four, the entire series being written between 2005 and 2008.

Other Bond authors have stretched 007's life in the opposite direction, making him somewhat older, yet Higson's work represented a wonderfully new 'take' on a very familiar subject. Having completed the series, and made the spy-thriller genre relevant to adolescents, Higson went on to do the same in another traditionally adult field, by penning a number of children's horror stories.

Odd man out
Sebastian Faulks, the
'serious' novelist

Sebastian Faulks (1953–) has been seen as the odd-man-out among the new Bond authors, in that he is chiefly known as a 'serious' novelist rather than a specialist in thrillers. Nevertheless he seems to have enjoyed writing *Devil May Care,* a classic Cold War adventure set in the Middle East.

He made a point of picking up where Fleming left off – in the familiar world of 1960s East-West confrontation – and his 007 is of the same ilk as the one who fought

Sebastian Faulks

Scaramanga in *The Man With the Golden Gun.* This Bond has the trappings and lifestyle – the smoking and drinking – that fans recalled, although he clearly fits uncomfortably into the atmosphere of 'swinging London'. Living, as he does, just off the legendary King's Road in Chelsea, he is nevertheless surprised by the smell of marijuana, a scent he associates with North African bazaars. Co-existing uneasily with the world of the Beatles, Faulks' Bond seems heartily relieved to escape abroad on a mission that lacks nothing in the pace and excitement of other adventures.

A GOOD STRETCH
In Sebastian Faulks' novel **Devil May Care,** *published in 2008 and set in the 1960s, M takes up yoga. This is neither the first nor the last time that the Bond stories stretch the bounds of credibility…*

Hooked
The contemporary Jeffery Deaver

Jeffrey Deaver (1950–) is the second US Bond author. An accomplished writer of thrillers who had produced 28 novels by the time he received a commission from Ian Fleming Publications Ltd, he has a reputation as more intellectual than authors in this action-centred field usually are, and is known for multiple plot twists. A native of Illinois, he was born in 1950 and had a distinctly promising start when, at the age of eight, he read a Bond book and was hooked. Three years later he even wrote, for his own amusement, a story – naturally of a somewhat derivative nature – about a British spy.

His more recent work on the subject – the Bond novel *Carte Blanche* – was published in 2011. The character he has created is thoroughly up-to-date (he has just served a tour in Afghanistan with the Armed Forces) and the references, as well as the equipment, the clothes and the language, are those of the present generation. This is a notable difference between Deaver's work and that of Sebastian Faulks or Charlie Higson, who enjoyed reviving a more dated feel in their narratives. This novel's launch, held at the spectacular St Pancras Hotel in London, included a suitably exciting moment – Deaver was handed the first copy of the book by a team of Royal Marines that had abseiled off the roof.

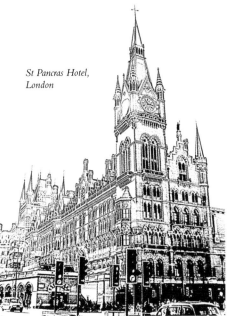

St Pancras Hotel, London

Permanent home
Fleming's legacy located in Indiana

Fleming's collection of volumes on the history of science, assembled by his bookseller friend Percy Muir in the 1930s as an investment for the author, was sold after his death by his wife, Ann. Included with this collection were the original drafts of 11 of his 14 Bond novels comprising stacks of typewritten pages that the author had had bound with buckram. The entire collection was bought by the University of Indiana at Bloomington, USA.

A midwestern state, with which Fleming had no connection and which was far removed from his European–Caribbean axis, may seem an unlikely resting place for his original workings. Surely the University of the West Indies, headquartered in Jamaica, would have been more suitable? In fact, the University of Indiana at Bloomington has, in its Lilly Library, one of the Western Hemisphere's greatest depositories of rare books. Its collection includes over 400,000 books and over 6.5 million manuscripts. Even the

Lilly Library, University of Indiana, USA

notoriously snobbish Fleming need not have felt completely disdainful of being held in such company.

The author's work in the Library is listed under the exhaustive title *The Ian Fleming Collection of Nineteenth and Twentieth Century Material Concerning Western Civilisation Together With the Original James Bond 007 Tales* and numbers over 1,000 volumes. Included are works on aviation, medicine, electricity, anthropology, communications and horticulture. Typical of them is a first edition of Charles Darwin's *The Origin of Species*; less typical are several books about particular sports, and a first edition of Robert Baden-Powell's seminal *Scouting for Boys*.

Muir assembled these volumes for Fleming over a period of about five years, after which the novelist's interest waned in developing his collection further. Fleming made some attempt to add to his scientific purchases – again in the form of first editions – by acquiring representative examples of the great works of literature from the same period. His collection therefore contained some valuable books by

Byron, Goethe, Dickens, Tolstoy and Kipling, and even an early edition of Adolf Hitler's *Mein Kampf*.

The public first viewed some of Fleming's scientific titles during an exhibition in London in 1963, and the University of Indiana bought the entire collection after negotiation through the book dealers Elkin Matthews Ltd, of which Fleming's friend Percy Muir was still a director.

Ann Fleming, distraught after her husband's death, agreed to the sale and was probably rather pleased to witness the departure of her husband's extensive book collection. The long shelves of these volumes, in their fleece-lined black bindings, had given their home a rather sombre appearance. She asked Muir to help her pack the materials for shipment, but when he arrived to do so she abruptly announced that she had changed her mind and did not want to part with them. A contract had already been signed, however, and she had no choice but to go ahead as planned with the sale.

The Lilly Library acquired, along with this collection, the lion's share of Fleming's Bond typescripts. As a former journalist he was accustomed to composing copy directly on to a typewriter and he had thus created no handwritten drafts, although the typed pages often carried his own scribbled comments. The Library holds typescripts for the following Fleming novels: *Casino Royale, Live and Let Die, Moonraker, Diamonds Are Forever, From Russia With Love, Dr No, Goldfinger, For Your Eyes Only, A View to a Kill, On Her Majesty's Secret Service* and *You Only Live Twice*.

Fleming's personal copies of at least six printed novels, again often with his own handwritten observations in the margins, and some uncorrected proofs are also included in the collection. To his own archive the Library have added the papers assembled by John Pearson when writing his biography of Fleming, along with the texts of more than 80 interviews about Fleming carried out among the author's friends. The catalogue of the University's Fleming Collection may be viewed online, and any researcher can apply for access to the materials it holds. For anyone with a serious interest in the life and work of Ian Fleming, all roads lead to Bloomington!

'Keep Bond British'
Will 007 always be British?

A lthough *Keep Bond British* was the title of a newspaper-led campaign that sought to influence the choice of a new actor, there has been no serious doubt that a suitable candidate from elsewhere could credibly play the role, and the producers have never thought in terms of nationality. While Englishmen (Moore and Craig), an Irishman (Brosnan), a Scotsman (Connery) and a Welshman (Dalton) have all played the agent, George Lazenby was of course Australian.

Several US actors have been considered for the role: Clint Eastwood (who felt the part should go to a British actor), Tom Sellek and John Gavin who was actually signed up to play Bond in *Diamonds Are Forever* before Sean Connery was persuaded to return. It is worth mentioning, too, that the first portrayal of the agent on screen – in a television adaptation of *Casino Royale* made in 1954 – was played by a US actor named Barry Nelson. Perhaps this does not count, however, since the programme was made by CBS and the agent was rewritten as an American character.

The movies are clearly too popular to allow the genre to die out, and suitable candidates will continue to be scouted for perhaps generations to come. Every decade or so, as the actor playing 007 retires through having become too old for the part or too tired of the 'stereotyping', it is safe to say that there will be another search for young men with the height, the looks and the manner to take on what is one of the most coveted roles in the acting profession. The right one could be anywhere.

Tom Sellek

Role of honour
Bond novels and movies

NOVELS BY IAN FLEMING

Casino Royale (1953)
Live and Let Die (1954)
Moonraker (1955)
Diamonds Are Forever (1956)
From Russia With Love (1957)
Dr No (1958)
Goldfinger (1959)
For Your Eyes Only (1960)
Thunderball (1961)
The Spy Who Loved Me (1962)
*On Her Majesty's Secret
Service* (1963)
You Only Live Twice (1964)
*The Man With the
Golden Gun* (1965)
Octopussy (1966)

NOVELS BY ROBERT MARKHAM (KINGSLEY AMIS)

Colonel Sun (1969)

NOVELS BY JOHN GARDNER

Licence Renewed (1981)
For Special Services (1982)
Icebreaker (1983)
Role of Honour (1984)
Nobody Lives Forever (1986)

No Deals, Mr Bond (1987)
Scorpius (1988)
Win, Lose or Die (1989)
Licence to Kill (1989)
Brokenclaw (1990)
The Man From Barbarossa (1991)
Death is Forever (1992)
Never Send Flowers (1993)
Seafire (1994)
GoldenEye (1995)
Cold (1996)

NOVELS BY RAYMOND BENSON

Zero Minus Ten (1997)
The Facts of Death (1998)
High Time to Kill (1999)
Doubleshoot (2000)
Never Dream of Dying (2001)
*The Man With the Red
Tattoo* (2002)
Union Trilogy (2008)
Choice of Weapons (2010)

NOVELS BY SEBASTIAN FAULKES

Devil May Care (2008)

NOVELS BY JEFFREY DEAVER

Carte Blanche (2011)

NOVELS BY CHARLIE HIGSON

Silverfin (2005)
Blood Fever (2006)
Double or Die (2007)
Hurricane Gold (2007)
By Royal Command (2008)

MOVIES

Dr No (1962)
From Russia With Love (1963)
Goldfinger (1964)
Thunderball (1965)
You Only Live Twice (1967)
Casino Royale (spoof) (1967)
*On Her Majesty's Secret
Service* (1969)
Diamonds Are Forever (1971)
Live and Let Die (1973)
*The Man With the
Golden Gun* (1974)
The Spy Who Loved Me (1977)
Moonraker (1979)
For Your Eyes Only (1981)
Octopussy (1983)
Never Say Never Again (1983)
A View to a Kill (1985)
The Living Daylights (1987)
Licence to Kill (1989)
GoldenEye (1995)
Tomorrow Never Dies (1997)
The World is Not Enough (1999)

Die Another Day (2002)
Casino Royale (2006)
Quantum of Solace (2008)
Skyfall (2012)

INDEX

MORE
AMAZING TITLES

LOVED THIS BOOK?

Tell us what you think and you could win another fantastic book from David & Charles in our monthly prize draw.

www.lovethisbook.co.uk

AMAZING & EXTRAORDINARY FACTS: LONDON
STEPHEN HALLIDAY
ISBN: 978-0-7153-3910-7

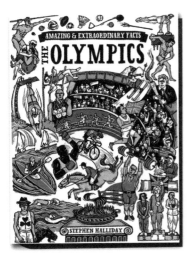

AMAZING & EXTRAORDINARY FACTS: OLYMPICS
STEPHEN HALLIDAY
ISBN: 978-1-4463-0201-9

AMAZING & EXTRAORDINARY FACTS: TITANIC
STUART ROBERTSON
ISBN: 978-1-4463-0194-4

PICTURE CREDITS

P26 © Tony Richards

P31 © Edward Hands

P37 © Pumpmeup

P39 © Andrew Dunn. http://
www.andrewdunnphoto.com/

P40 © Alexander Z

P41 © BrokenSphere

P46 © Iain Crump

P52 © EzykronHD

P63 © Richard Hebstreit

P75 © Vexillus

P77 © TheArmadillo

P94 © Matthew Field, http://www.
photography.mattfield.com

P99 © Benchill

P100 © Mike Peel (www.
mikepeel.net).

P102 © Bundesarchiv, B 145
Bild-F015892-0010 / Wegmann,
Ludwig / CC-BY-SA

P106 © http://www.adamsguns.com

P120 © Bsodmike

P127 © Vladimir Vyatkin/
Владимир Вяткин

P130 © Przemysław Sakrajda

P134 © Parrot of Doom

P135 © Alan Light

P143 © http://www.adamsguns.com/

FURTHER INFORMATION

THE JAMES BOND INTERNATIONAL FAN CLUB,

PO BOX 21,

York YO41 1WX

United Kingdom

Tel: (0900-1700) +44 1347 878837

Fax: +44 1347 878839

General Enquiries: David Black

davidblack@007.info

Membership Enquiries:

membership@007.info